WILD
BUSINESS

Awaken To Your Feminine Force To Launch
Your Business On Your Own Terms

SIGOURNEY BELLE

Wild Business
By Sigourney Belle
This work is exclusively published and facilitated by Beverly Hills Publishing
468 Camden Drive, Beverly Hills, CA 90210
www.beverlyhillspublishing.com

Copyright © 2021, Sigourney Belle. All rights reserved.

ISBN: 978-1-7360900-4-6

This book is dedicated to Mother Earth; my own mother; & my unborn child, due September 2021.

It is dedicated to my next chapter, bringing a child into this world – a gift of new eyes and fresh sight and to the innocence and purity of the children that walk this earth. It is dedicated to birth, the deepest act of courage and surrender to the feminine and the body.

This book is dedicated to love.

Table of Contents

PREFACE
The Earth is Calling You Home

To her wetness.
Her wildness.
To the lifeblood of ecstasy and the river of love that pours to
and through you.
She is calling you home to move you.
To dance with you.
To remind you that this life is worth living.
No longer will you be able to show up for a job
In four concrete walls
That leaches you dry
Of all that you came to offer
No, the world wants you dripping
Melting
Opening
She wants all of you
And she is ready
Can you hear her call?
The Earth is calling you home.
Your body is asking you to listen

To the richness of life that is waiting for you
Maybe you can feel it
Your life as you once knew it to be
Is changing
Things are not going to look the same, moving forwards
The power structures that have held rigid and that have controlled
the wild, unstoppable life force that lives in the bodies of humanity
Are falling
Our souls will no longer allow us to stay trapped
And confined
In a life that is not truly our own
In a life that does not permit us the freedom
To fully feel
The depth of what life has to offer.
This is Wild Business™.
It is not just a book.
It offers you an alternative
And teaches you how to dive head first
Into the mysteries of creation
To birth yourself into the world
from soul
And to trust
That something greater than yourself has got you
You just have to take the first step
Move and the path will open for you
There is a whole world in front of you that is ready for you to explore

Do you trust in the darkness?
In the space of the unknown?
The traditional ways of doing business are over
The power structures can no longer survive
They are devoid of soul
And are extracting energy that is not already there
But the Earth will no longer allow us to keep living this way.
This is why we are in another socioeconomic collapse.
And the work of connecting back to the Earth begins with first
learning how to connect with our own bodies.
By learning how to listen
To what is deeper:
The voice of our intuition
This is syntropy
And if we all start to live this way
And create from the deep web that draws us silently to where
we are meant to go
Then we will always be provided with what we need.
It is time for cultural and evolutionary change.
Because we cannot keep going the way that we have been.
The Earth is calling us home.

INTRODUCTION
Welcome to Wild Business™

Can you imagine building a wildly successful, profitable business from the ground up, with nothing but trust, intuition, and the skills to serve clients with your gifts?

This is how I did it.

When I left my last formal job, I had no idea how to start, grow, or build a business, let alone scale it. I didn't have any kind of "coach" to dictate what to do.

One step after the other, I danced with the unknown, I listened, and I followed my impulses, even when I was shaking with fear.

All I had was a willing heart and a deep connection to stillness, and the ability to feel the pulse of my own life force as it showed me where from and where to...

...and as if by magic, I birthed two six-figure businesses in three years – with no strategy, no plan, and no massive corporate structure.

The truth is, I don't even have a background in business or entrepreneurship.

Yet I've published books, travelled all over the world, developed my own healing modality, and taught hundreds of people in my trainings. The launch of this book is yet another wave of expansion for my business, and just like everything else, it has happened just like magic.

I created an Empire, and I want to help you to do the same.

Not an Empire like it's been done before.

Not one based upon power and control structures.

But one where you understand the inherent genius in those you are working with and can elevate them into their own genius and sovereignty to support your vision.

Because most businesses rely on a central power and control mechanism that suppresses the feminine principles of intuition, emotion, receptivity, deep feeling, creativity, and connection.

My mission here is to restore these principles back into business models and to create communities that allow for syntropy and sustainability.

To build empires that support nature's desires for organic growth, flow, and ecstatic creation.

Because the old ways of doing things are dead.

It's no longer possible to push down your own needs and desires to run a business that feels devoid of life force and that keeps you trapped.

You deserve more.

And that's why I created Wild Business™.

Because your business can be wildly alive and feel ecstatic like nature if you learn how to listen to the laws of creation and move WITH the energy of where the business is wanting to go.

It's all energetics.

And wherever your business is stuck, it's because there is something stuck either within you, your team, or your life.

With the tools I teach, you learn how to develop pinpoint intuition to hone in on any stuck areas, as well as the ability to clear the energetics within your business. A Wild Business™ is thriving, flowing, and growing – one that can be scaled organically and without force.

We have deeply rooted ideas of what a business needs to look like, and most of those are incompatible with our true nature as sensitive, intuitive, feeling beings.

It's our disconnection from this natural sensitivity, which has created an epidemic of burnout, exhaustion, exploitation of our life force. It's what makes it so hard to do business in the current paradigm.

If you've struggled with the sterility of the corporate world, know that it's not your fault – these business models have been built to burn you out. We live in a world full of distractions and "shoulds," driven by capitalism and an attention-sucking economy.

On a societal level, we're unplugged from and disconnected from the divine and our spiritual path. We've been programmed with the drive to generate income and survive, to gain power and material success for ourselves alone, to feed a corporate beast that doesn't care for the human condition. The ideals of the feminine and the sustainable qualities of connection, intuition and empathy are largely devoid in the current business paradigm.

I worked in the medical industry, moving from one hospital to the next for 8 years, and was mortified at how clients are treated like subjects, not people. Health was treated as something to "fix," instead of human beings as something to love and tend to and nourish.

Instead of getting to the root of the source of the pain, we cover it up with bandaids and medications.

But what is the real issue at hand, when we see a society where people are sick, tired, and wondering what the point of it all is?

The real issue is that we have forgotten who we are.

We have forgotten our true nature.

We have forgotten how to dance, to sing, to live and breathe in harmony with the Earth and her cycles.

How to return to the simple medicines of connection and laughter.

It takes a funeral to bring families together.

A wedding or birthday to cause any kind of celebration.

And yet that kind of deep emotional connection is available to us every day.

We simply need to start putting our humanity at the forefront, to choose to move beyond the masks, and to drop deeper – to awaken our feminine.

When I speak of feminine or masculine, I'm not speaking about male or female biology, but rather about the qualities of the two. Our feminine nature is the part of us that is intuitively connected, compassionate, emotional, is connected to our bodies, and the part of us that inherently desires love, to be loved and to give love.

The masculine nature is more of an action-oriented energy, the penetrative part of us that desires to show up and be of service to the world; a more outwardly state.

All human beings have these dual aspects within us.

These qualities are inherent in all genders, no matter what the biological makeup. Just as the feminine is often depicted as the earth, the mother, the land that nourishes and cares for us, the masculine is depicted as the sky – our cosmic connection to the heavens, our astral bodies, and our non-physical universe.

Night and day.

Summer and winter.

Light and dark.

They are two sides of the coin, neither better or worse, right or wrong.

We are currently experiencing the fourth wave of feminism, which many say was catalysed in December 2012 when a young woman was brutally gang-raped in India and subsequently died. This sparked a huge international wave of activism with rape culture being the central focus.

I believe that this wave of feminism is not just about the reclamation of the feminine; it is about returning to balance; returning to the soul.

The soul does not know right or wrong; it doesn't even know feminine or masculine.

It is the divine, infinite expression that only knows the taste of its own ecstatic wonder.

Like the child who looks around in awe at the magic of being alive.

The soul is beyond polarity.

Beyond right or wrong.

But in order for us to experience the taste of soul emerging, we need to first accept and acknowledge that which has been buried and hidden in our own psyches as well as the collective psyche.

And a lot of what has been buried has been related to our feminine nature.

The part of us that is totally wild, awake, ecstatic, and utterly out of control.

The part of us that cannot be tamed. And will not be tamed.

The part of us that desires to be ravished by love.

To wake up every day and curiously move through life and create without an agenda and without having to box ourselves into four walls at a computer.

The feminine is a gateway to the soul, and we are moving into an era of soul-led business – where we embrace the totality of our human condition and fully express our sensitivity, divinity, and spiritual gifts.

The corporate model we grew up with was built around the patriarchal and martial systems of war, control, and power. It wasn't built to work with the cycles of the Earth, or with our inherent energy resources. And it certainly was never designed to support the flourishing of our individual creative genius.

Our genius – our highest aligned expression of our gifts and talents – is often suppressed, suffocated, and in some cases, even punished by the system itself. Reconnecting with our harmonized nature through the gateway of the feminine is the only way for us to create a business model that truly serves our soul.

In some of my trainings I talk about unleashing the Queen within us. The archetype of the Queen is a woman who is living her highest spiritual purpose, represented by her crown. When we're living in alignment with our creative genius, we're living as that archetype of the Queen. Queen energy overrides the notion that there's anything actually wrong with us.

Throughout this book, I'll be sharing the practices that I work within my own life to unleash the Queen in me; the full force of my feminine power and creativity. This feminine force has a life of its own. It speaks to and guides you where it wants your business to go.

Wild Business™ is a path of self-initiation; where you give yourself full permission to let go of any formal business structure that doesn't work for you and move from the seat of divine feminine power. It is a way of doing business that feels relaxed, effortless, magical, soulful, and natural.

You don't need a blueprint or a strategy to create a potent and profitable business, and I'm not going to give you one in this book.

I'm not going to teach you how to come up with a company name, choose fonts and colours, or set up your back-end accounting system.

In this book, you'll receive the transmission of my accredited modality, the Feminine Frequency Formula™, which I work with to ignite people's creative gifts and help them physically manifest the visions that want to come through them.

The Feminine Frequency Formula™ works across genders. It was originally called the parasympathetic restoration formula because it activates the parasympathetic state of the nervous system, responsible for rest, digestion, relaxation, and release of trauma and tension in the body. It takes us into deeper states of consciousness, where natural healing occurs.

This frequency is also where intuition turns on; it's where we feel more like ourselves, more connected to our bodies, more able to empathize with others, and more in tune with nature – which is our natural state of alignment.

We need to start coming into balance with the connected, empathic, and intuitive aspects of ourselves if we are going to run businesses that truly feel good for us, and for the planet.

A New Renaissance

I feel we're at the precipice of a massive cultural change.

At the time of publishing this book, we are experiencing a Saturn -Jupiter conjunction in Capricorn; the last major astrological alignment of 2020 representing the upheaval and overhaul of the societal power structures that are constricting the natural world – both within and without. As the world emerges from the threat of COVID, we have been forced to confront who and what is most important to us, and how we are all interconnected.

Rules are being rewritten as we reevaluate our lives, and I'm feeling that how we do business will change dramatically over the coming months.

I believe we are currently sitting in the Next Renaissance and the emergence of art and beauty as the new "business" paradigm.

I am here to support this movement of redefining business as we know it, so that it is based upon individual sovereignty, love, and freedom. I'm seeing a breakdown of the old hierarchical structures that kept us locked into lives and jobs that we don't actually want to be in. It is my belief that when you learn how to discover your creative genius and hear the voice of your intuition, you can create a business from that foundation that is thriving, organic, and authentic for you.

Why do I believe this?

Because I'm living this reality today.

My business is thriving and alive, shifting as my heart's desires shift, reaching solid levels of success in every avenue by following the creative energy that is constantly shifting, changing, and wild – just like nature.

When I say Wild Business™, I'm speaking of the wildness that we see in nature that's inherently alive and awake, and it's moving. What I desire is for you to have a business that feels good to your soul, and that feeds your energy to create.

We can create businesses without burnout, meaning that we have to be in sync with our bodies, our natural rhythms, and in touch with the magical state we see in children, where we are free of the conditioning of the mind that tells us what's right and what's wrong. There is so much sabotage inherent in that. This book is an invitation to return to that quality of wildness, and discover how we can drop back into that natural state of curiosity and aliveness that drives us to make an impact in the world with our business.

Business is Medicine

I didn't intend to head down the path of entrepreneurship originally; everything I teach about business is self-learned.

I struggled with the schooling system, but was drawn to the medical field where I became a senior neurological physiotherapist. At age 23, I had a huge turning point after suffering a complete psychological and emotional breakdown. I was diagnosed with multiple health issues, but nothing got to the core of what was happening to me. All I knew was I was extremely stressed.

Ironically, I was diagnosing clients with neurological disorders and I began manifesting some of the symptoms I saw in my clients. No one could offer me any solutions. At the time, I was in amazing shape – I was an elite athlete and had been training for the world titles in Karate. I was seeing psychologists, I was working with dietary changes, but nothing in my head changed.

I went from being extremely fit to not being able to walk up a set of stairs; it was as if I couldn't lift my feet off the ground. It led to me having a complete breakdown, which is when I had a huge awakening and my vision opened.

That's when I started to be able to see clearly what was ahead of me. I chose to let go of the life I was told I should live. I went to Nepal to study and live in a Buddhist monastery and started studying Tibetan Buddhism and The Lam Rim, The Buddhist Teachings of the Path to Enlightenment. I also lived in India for a year and studied through various ashrams. From that point onwards, I had clear sight about what my purpose was. When I returned from India, I went back into the medical model, but this time working holistically. I started integrating energetic work and the modalities I was teaching into my work as a physiotherapist.

Something was very different this time; it was as if I was actually able to hear and know what was happening in someone's body before I walked into a hospital room to meet with a client.

There are multiple examples of this, but the last person I saw as a medical patient is what changed my perspective more towards what I call "business medicine."

The last client I saw in the medical system came to me with chronic neurological pain in both of her legs, bilateral numbness. Medical scans showed nothing, but she had very real symptoms – she could barely walk. I tuned into her energy and explained that I saw her painting in a home on the ocean. I didn't sense where her pain was coming from, but I shared what I was feeling about her. She had a complete emotional breakdown in front of me. She shared that six years prior, she quit being an artist and a painter, which was her absolute joy and passion job, and instead went into a "normal" job.

After one of our sessions, she decided to go back to painting and she moved into a home on the coast. Soon her symptoms dissolved and I started to see that the physical symptoms at the root was a spiritual block. There was some kind of block to this person's truth.

I firmly believe by looking at the root of that disconnect from her spirit, and making a change that aligned with her creative genius, that her body was able to resolve its physical symptoms on its own.

This is where the idea of Business Medicine came from, and I started offering business medicine sessions in my private practice. Business medicine is the foundational philosophy of Wild Business.™

Business medicine is based upon the idea that business is medicine for the soul. Our soul's work is what provides us with deep spiritual fulfilment and nourishment. Not only that, but all of our physical, mental, and psychospiritual issues come from a root disconnection from spirit and when we align our paths to devote ourselves to what wants to move through us and how we are best of service to the world, then we have a business that is always going to be abundantly fruitful and rewarding at all levels.

There hasn't been a business school for mystics, psychics, empaths, spiritual healers, or the highly intuitive – until now.

And in this school, you are the teacher.

Absorb what information serves you, and discard what doesn't. Always follow your intuition above all.

Wild Business™ is a way of dropping into a state of intuitive awareness and learning how to communicate with your business on a subtle level. When you do that, it becomes very easy to run a business, but not in a formulaic way; rather, your business speaks to you.

In the time I grew my business to be six figures in just a year, with three employees, I never once had a business mentor.

My business moves and the direction I took all came through to me whilst in deep meditative spaces, where I was communicating with the spirit of my business and asking it what it needed to drive it forwards.

My only job has been to get out of my own way and to listen and action what has been shown to me. I want to teach you how to do the same, as I believe that this is the missing piece for entrepreneurs at this time on Earth.

When we don't listen, we have to come up with answers ourselves using our logical minds. This requires far more effort than to be in a receptive state and to RECEIVE the answers.

In the new paradigm and the age that we are currently living in, we are being asked to step out of our heads and to learn how to navigate life more intuitively – to deeply listen to energy.

The guidance in this book, whilst it will help you to connect with the soul of your business, will also open you up to being more deeply attuned to its essence so that you can receive information effortlessly.

Through these skills, you will be able to download the core message of your genius, your brand, and your business without any external aid.

If you have been feeling like saying goodbye to the traditional way of doing things, and creating a business from the fire of your intuition and the magic of your vision, this is your permission slip.

Welcome back to the wild.

CHAPTER ONE
Nature Origins

I grew up in nature on a small island off the coast of Western Australia, called North Island, which is a part of the Abrolhos group – a small group of 122 islands in the Indian Ocean.

No shops, no cars.

Just the spaciousness of island life & community.

I have spent most of my life trying to retrieve that feeling of home; to reconnect to the infinite current that I feel when I'm dancing in the forest or swimming in the seas.

I spent my childhood immersed in my imagination and my inner world. My mum would always say I was either creating, and wouldn't let anyone near me, or I was telling everyone what to do. As well as being highly creative, I was an extremely sensitive child, and I faced a lot of trouble when I went into the schooling system.

There was not a single part of me that could conform. I was extremely rebellious at school; I hated being told what to do. I was always jumping on tables, taking my clothes off, and running around naked. In music class, I'd have to sit in the corner, tapping the triangle, because I wasn't allowed to play the instruments as I'd just go off on my own and disrupt the class. I was always being really, really naughty, and that's because I literally could not stand being confined to anyone else's ideologies.

In my later years of schooling, I realized that the way that I absorbed information was very different from others. Traditional learning was just frustrating for me.

I had a photographic memory and could download information about something just by looking at it. Later, I could access that information if I needed to. It was like osmosis; I absorbed knowledge through frequency, through my body, in a way that was beyond the mind's intelligence. And so, I could never sit and listen to lectures, because I knew there was a quicker way to learn.

I'd think, "I can learn that in two seconds, and you're taking hours to explain it; it doesn't make any sense." Ironically, I got the top marks out of everyone, even though I would never listen to any of the teachings.

Like many highly sensitive children, I was categorized with all kinds of mental and psychological disorders; labeled with severe depression, potential bipolar disease, and anxiety. Inside me, I never felt that there was something wrong with me, even though everyone told me there was.

When I hit the age of 15, I went through a massive mental, spiritual, emotional, psychological breakdown that lasted through to my 23rd birthday. Seven years of being in a deep process of suffering. I hardly left my room. I was just very internal. I didn't think there was anything wrong apart from the fact that I was being reflected back to by everyone on the outside I was being depressed. I was quite comfortable.

I did have a sense of grief, for sure, and this sense of dissociation from the world. I did not feel like I could be in physical reality. That's because during this period of time I was realizing, "I don't feel like I'm like everyone else actually; I don't fit into this model and way of being in society, and I don't really have any examples or frameworks for what does work for me."

There was nothing that I could see that was pointing me into a direction that felt like it resonated with who I was and what I wanted to do. It was a period of awakening, of first realizing that I needed to feel the deep discomfort of, "I don't fit in with these models. I have to create something of my own." I was driven by the discomfort.

By the time I got to age 23, I was in the medical industry, and I was stressed. After seven years of seeing psychologists and seeing physicians and trying every diet under the sun, exercising, all the things that should help with these kinds of states, I was out of effective options. Anything I'd try would work for a little bit and then I'd hit a block and then sink back down.

I didn't like the industry I was in and I just didn't know what I wanted to be doing. That was when I had my first experience of a complete meltdown.

In that moment, I just felt like I needed to ask. I was by no means religious, but I felt like I needed to pray and I did.

I put my hands in prayer and rested them on my forehead and I asked, "If there's something bigger, if there's any form of guidance that wants to come through for me right now, please do. I'm completely stuck."

In that moment, my psychic vision opened up. I saw this map before me, a timeline, which some people would call the Akashic records. It was almost like a video that was playing out, where I was walking through all of these different stages of my life and I saw where I was going.

I was like, "Whoa." I just knew something was about to change.

The first thing I had seen in my vision was me standing at these massive monastery gates. Two weeks later, I was on social media on Facebook and someone put up a post about a monastery that they lived and studied in. I felt the impulse to apply, got in, and six months later I was living and studying in a Tibetan Buddhist monastery over in Nepal.

Over the next 10 years, I was living in ashrams in India, studying yoga therapy and learning the ways of various esoteric and ancient wisdom. Then later, I walked the Tantric path for some years. Then it was back to the Western medical industry, seeing the disparity of the two again and then realizing I was a medical intuitive. Through my esoteric studies, I'd done so much work on opening myself up receptively that when I went back into society, I was able to scan people's bodies and know exactly what was happening with them.

Then I broke away from the medical industry and I started doing more holistic work and energy work, more frequency work actually. Whilst I was doing medical intuitive work, it was mainly just tracking energy and freeing people's blocks out, which would help them heal spiritually. I wasn't necessarily saying to people, "You've got a kidney stone," even though that is something that I could test for. That didn't interest me.

I could feel that and I could tell them that if I wanted to, but my passion was that I wanted to free them of what was happening. To get to the root of their illness and discover what was underneath it. And then to support them in moving past it. Often I didn't need to share what was happening for them and that would have been a distraction. Instead, I let the frequencies I work with do the work and they come to their own conclusions. That also stops me from stepping into "saviour" and being another reason for someone to rely on something external to them to "fix" them.

Since breaking free of the systems that kept my own intuition at bay, I have been in flow with the ecstatic current of life- nature. This has provided me with all of the answers I have needed along the way to grow an organic business that is awake, alive, and that nourishes me.

One of the keys is surrender.

Every time I've been stuck, every time I feel like there's been a block and I've been trying to forge my path forwards, I've sat back and I've just asked. I've been like, "What is it that I need to know? Where do I need to go?" And something lands, I see something and it takes me on this next thread. My life is about following these threads into the next opportunity and the next.

Throughout this book, I talk a lot about dying to the dark and trusting the mystery. These are ways of expressing that we have to be okay with not knowing and not needing to know, and actually allow something bigger to work through us. When we humble ourselves enough to know that we are being guided, we find a more seamless way to navigate life and do business.

This is a key issue at the foundation of the way business and society is currently set up – it doesn't teach us, from childhood, how to listen within. We are redirected away from our intuition, away from our inner teacher, and into the lecture hall, where an older, supposedly wiser authority transmits ideas and knowledge to us. I'm all for formulas, blueprints, history, and structure that serves us, but to deny our inherent intelligence or try to force it to look or behave a certain way has never boded well for me.

Children are wise and inherently connected to their wildness. We are greatly shaped by what happens in our childhood, especially between the ages of 0-7 when our primal brain is the main driver and our cognitive logic (our prefrontal cortex) is still being formed, making our minds very impressionable. This means that until we're seven years old, everyone else's voices become the imprints in our subconscious mind. These imprints drive our behaviour and our conscious thought. If we were imprinted to believe we were incapable, unloveable, or unworthy, we'll find that in our business today, we're simply not able to sell, market, or launch anything that will fill the emotional void caused by that trauma.

The inner child is the part of us that is eternally in curiosity, wonder, and sensitivity. It is the part of us that is pure, intuitive, and creative by nature. Your inner child holds the key to unlocking the potential of your creative genius.

In my trainings, I help people go back to these deeply rooted emotional memories and release them so that the inner child can come fully online and start to play and create, the way it was meant to.

Most importantly, we need to adopt these lessons for ourselves, today.

This is important for our journey because ultimately, we must give this gift to our own inner child – playing the role of the supportive, encouraging parent that we always needed. We must teach our inner child to trust their own voice, as opposed to imprinting external belief systems onto ourselves, which then become our overriding voice of wisdom.

We must learn how to guide ourselves back to our own sovereign understanding of how to listen, and how to respond to our bodies. How to be as we naturally are.

All of us are, naturally, deeply sensitive.

When we give our nervous systems a chance to work with the cycles of nature, we experience more ease, more joy, more contentment, and a greater sense of relaxation in our everyday lives.

As a society, however, we have dissociated from our natural sensitivity – which means we're also dissociated from nature. Trauma, to me, is the dissociation from our natural state.

When we live without addressing our nervous systems and our sensitivity, we create unhealthy patterns that manifest in our business.

For the most part, we grow up addicted to stress.

And so we also respond to stress.

Most of us are born in hospitals with heavily medicated mothers who are disconnected from feeling the natural ecstasy – the pain and pleasure – of birth.

And then from that point, we start living our lives avoiding pain in the pursuit of pleasure-hedonism.

We will NEVER live stress-free, fulfilling lives if we are always looking to avoid suffering in the pursuit of what is shiny and bright.

But we're conditioned to be drawn to that which is shiny – which is also founded on feeding our pattern of constantly needing more.

Of needing to be constantly stressed.

Because here's the thing – most people are afraid of NOT being stressed.

Because what's underneath that?

True feeling.

Deep feeling.

AND

That's also where our true self is revealed.

The old paradigm makes you believe that your essential nature is wrong and that you need to be fixed.

The old feeds off your stress and leaves you dry and feeling like you still need more.

The new paradigm?

Shows you how to unlearn all of it and drop deeply into yourself... to find what you were always looking for that CANNOT be found...

The part of you that's already whole.

Reconnection with our sensitivity is key, and in this book I'm going to show you exactly how you can do that.

Consider these questions:

How often do you take yourself out simply to be in nature?

Do you play outside? What does that look like for you?

Do you spend any time in the forest, with trees, or in a garden?

When was the last time you visited, touched, or swam in the ocean?

What are your favourite things to observe in Nature?

Have you put your bare feet on the Earth today?

When was the last time you gave yourself a full day away from your phone and simply existed in the natural world?

These questions are here to spark your awareness of your current relationship with nature. I don't necessarily believe we need to be on the Earth every single day in order to feel connected to Nature – we are always connected, even when we're at work. But if we're feeling severely out of balance or depleted in this area, we can immediately start making shifts by connecting with nature in the physical.

Maybe you've been craving a weekend camping trip or have been fantasizing about renting a cabin in the woods to work on your book. Perhaps you've been getting a feeling to relocate entirely to a new environment.

Getting in touch with nature is what we need to do individually to move forward so that each individual can be part of this collective uprising of harmony on Earth.

Right now, the most critical thing we can do is to eliminate stress from our lives.

When I worked in the hospital system, I was in such a heightened state of stress. Me – a highly sensitive individual with ESP – was running a 35-bed ward, by myself, as a new grad with no assistance, surrounded by people running around in a constant state of emergency. I'd literally get to work, vomit in the toilets, and head to see my first patient.

At the end of the day, it felt like I had to literally extract myself from the stress and physically move my body into a space of nature. I'd head straight to the beach and walk until I could feel my heart again. Or I'd go to the pine forest opposite the hospital, lay on the earth, and just breathe. I used to work a lot with plant medicines as well; I find them so intuitive and wise. I would take a microdose of mushrooms, lay on the earth, and just allow my body to relax and become attuned to the earth. I'd let my emotional body run – cry, shake, feel, release – then sink into the Mother and feel my heartbeat becoming one with the earth.

In that state, I would start receiving so much energy, inspiration, activation, and guidance. I reconnected with my steady current and I reconnected with my heart, and I remembered who I was. Who we are is not something we can know – it's a felt sensation; a sense of the soul.

You know if your life and your work have been devoid of soul. There's a dullness to everything where you want to feel sparkle and shine. A heaviness and dread where you want to feel motivated and clear.

When we start to remove ourselves from stress, connect to our inner child, and be with the Earth, we remember our true nature – it's intuitive, free, alive, wild, creative, limitless, non-linear.

Returning to nature is the first step on the path of Wild Business™. It is a choice we must make in order to create a business that is syntropic, harmonious, and resonant with the deepest desires of our soul.

My invitation to you at the completion of this first chapter is to pause, close this book, and step outside. If you're already in nature, soak it up. Celebrate your connection. Take in your environment with fresh eyes, with an open mind. Appreciate the harmony that is flowing all around you, within you, and through you. Breathe it in. Let it out. Receive.

As you are about to learn, the spirit of your business will dance with you in many subtle ways. It will communicate with you like the song on the breeze, like the patterns of the river flow.

Connecting with nature will help you open the portal to the creative genius that wants to come through you.

CHAPTER TWO
Opening the Portal

I magine this: your business is alive, and waiting to meet you. It has a soul, a personality, and a voice. It has colour, shape, form, and texture. It knows exactly who you need to contact, what you need to do, and where you need to go next in order to bring it through the portal of your vision and into waking life.

In many ways, I treat business like shamanism. When I work with a business – my own, or another's – I access the spirit of the business and have communication with it, just like shamans commune with spirits and energies "across the veil." It is an act of connecting with the unseen web of Creation that is ever-flowing and manifesting into our reality.

All of us can do this.

This chapter is about unlocking your natural ability to connect with the unseen realms and start a relationship with the essence of your business. Opening up to this type of relationship with your business creates an opportunity for you to receive insight and clarity that no step-by-step program will ever give you.

Most of us have been conditioned to believe and follow an external authority on what we should do. We try to stay safe and comfortable by playing within the rules and limits of this 3D reality. But the truth is, we have the capacity to create whatever our soul desires. We just have to be open to the magic, open to the mystery. Cultivating the humility and willingness to completely trust the mystery of life is the only way to create a business that is rooted in our highest callings – and deepest yearnings.

At the end of the day, what we deeply want is beyond $10k months and thousands of followers. Those things can happen, and they will, when we're vibrationally aligned with what we truly want – alive in our art, expressing our purpose, and living our best lives.

And so, your greatest asset on this journey will be your ability to dance with the mystery and surrender to the unknown. Life is unpredictable, and oftentimes, intuitive guidance seems to drop in at the eleventh hour. I don't know how many times I've received guidance to uproot my life, leave a relationship, move homes on short notice, or completely stop all forward momentum on a project. I often find myself resisting in those moments where I get the impulse, but every single time I listen and follow through, the reward is immediate and evident. I am always relieved when I trust my intuition and leap forward into the unknown.

Every business that I've created has come through me first as an intuitive feeling and a vision.

You are not your business. Your business is an entity of its own, with its own desires and needs. If you learn how to communicate with your business, it will show you what it needs, and you can tell it what you need, too. It is a partnership. The feelings of ease, flow, and expansion we wish to experience in business can only occur when we are connected to its spirit. If we are not, it will feel like we always have to push, or that things are hard. That's not to say that sometimes running a business doesn't require effort, because it certainly does. But it can feel like a flow of endless energy, it can feel nourishing, it can feel like it's empowering you.

Communicating with your business means that you can start to relate with it, get to know it, and nurture it. Sometimes the guidance you'll receive is to get more rest or have a warm meal. Sometimes it'll look like making a phone call or writing an email, and other times it'll look like taking a day in complete silence and meditation.

This type of communication is a two-way street – you can also make requests of your business, to honour your creative energy and boundaries. Setting a boundary with the spirit of your business can look like saying, "Hey, I'd prefer not to be woken up at 3:00 am with a whole heap of ideas. I'd rather receive inspiration in the mornings when I awake." I share this because a lot of clients I work with, who open the portal to their vision, often find themselves streaming creative ideas and energies to a point that is either inconvenient or exhausting.

When I was writing my book, Leviathan, the words were pouring through me at such a rapid rate that I couldn't do literally anything except write – no cooking, driving, interacting with the outside world – for a whole week.

Trust that you actually can communicate with your business on a non-physical level, and develop the relationship with the spirit of your business just like you would with a physical business partner.

Now, just like any relationship, spending time together is the only way to deepen your connection and strengthen your bond.

If you're in a job you're not fond of, and you're currently giving your time and attention to relationships or projects that aren't really aligned for you, it may feel difficult at first to make a commitment to this relationship with your Wild Business™. But in order for your business to give to you, you need to give to it. It is a symbiotic relationship.

Unless you have time and space dedicated to your creativity, it will not come through.

I have had people tell me before that they don't feel like their business was going to work, and when I tune into their business, it tells me that they are not putting the time into it.

I am all about ease, grace, and feminine flow – and yet I know that you cannot expect to succeed with anything if you don't put the energy into it.

YES, this path is about achieving all that you desire for yourself with ease and grace, but to experience that consistency of manifestation comes from a willingness to be in active partnership with your business, which is going to require your full investment and commitment.

It will also require you to make decisions that challenge and stretch your capacity.

What I can tell you for sure is, the more love you develop for your business, the greater you will be rewarded.

Your business wants to nourish you. It wants to work with you. It wants the path of least resistance for you, and it wants to help you thrive. You have not been singlehandedly picked out by the universe to suffer. And you certainly haven't been single-handedly picked out by your business not to succeed.

How can you prove this to yourself?

It's simple – surrender the idea that you know everything. If you're calling something in with your intellect, you're limited by what's been told to you. But the minute you say, "I don't know," you release the mind's control over you and you let the divine in to do its work.

I often hear myself say, "I have no fucking idea what I'm doing." This is true for all of us, but it really becomes obvious when you step into the realm of Wild Business™. No external system, authority figure, boss, or structure can carry you through the choices and decisions you need to make every single day as a sovereign entrepreneur.

What you can know, feel, and trust – and what you will feel by doing this work – is that you're being carried and supported by the mystery. That everything is working out for you. And that your business can truly reflect the greatness inside you.

As we step into the magical realms of the Wild Business™ practices, I encourage you to shift into a state of curiosity about what lies beyond your fear of the unknown.

The first practice I'm going to share with you is creating a sacred space, where you can be in your practice and use the tools that I'm going to share with you throughout this book. This space is different from your office or where you normally work. It could potentially be in your bedroom, or in another room where you are able to be undisturbed. What's most important are the energetic qualities of this space, as it provides the container for you to drop into the feminine darkness and receive guidance.

Creating Sacred Space

When setting up your space, it is important for it to be clean and minimal. Every object and piece of furniture in your space holds a vibrational frequency, and so the more objects you have in your space, the more energy and sensory input you are opening yourself up to.

The simpler the setup, the greater the energetic clarity.

To support your inner clarity, remove clutter from your room and home.

Ensure there are minimal objects in your sacred space.

Organize your essentials. Only keep items that feel significant to you, and release everything else.

As you let go of unneeded items, you're metaphysically releasing attachments to the stories, timelines, and identities that are linked to the clutter in your life – and you're making space for the new.

Another aspect of creating sacred space is creating personal boundaries or agreements with others that allow you to be alone in your sacred space. If you need to make arrangements with roommates or partners to be undisturbed, do so. I have been in situations where I've had to share my room with a partner and have needed to be extra vigilant in assuring I have solo time to dive into this work. In extreme circumstances, if you need to take yourself out to another location, into a private place in nature, do so.

Sacred space is a physical manifestation of your commitment to devote a part of your life to your soul work. This path of Wild Business™ is soul work – the process of learning who you are on the deepest level, and creating from there.

I use the word sacred because the essence of life truly is.

Everything is – including us, our vision, and the gifts that want to come through us.

Creating a Business Altar

An altar creates a portal. It is a point of access to other realms and information outside of yourself.

An altar raises the object of your attention into a position of focus so that you can direct your energy into it. The reason I invite you to create an altar for your business is not so that you worship your business or pray to it. Your business – and your bank account – is not a god to be idolized. The altar can help you tune into the essence of your business, which is like a flowing stream of creative ideas and energies. This is much like tuning in to a certain radio station to receive the frequencies being broadcast there.

What to use for an altar? In terms of a physical structure, you may have a nightstand, table, chest, windowsill, or shelf that will serve nicely. Even a small box, bowl, or tray will do.

Design your altar with items that inspire you and connect you to your heart. I suggest placing an item in each of the directions - north, east, south, west, as well as at the centre.

Bring nature in – water, crystals, fresh or dried flowers, leaves, branches, soil, or sand.

Candles are an important ritual tool (and my preferred source of lighting). The element of fire connects us to the spirit of death, rebirth, and purification – which is what we experience as we connect to higher states of creativity and consciousness.

I recommend acquiring three special candles for your business altar, representing the feminine, the masculine, and the divine union of the two.

Three is the Holy Trinity – this is the number that represents unity, harmony, and balance.

You can always change your altar as you desire.

Trust your intuition.

Basic Energetic Hygiene

We are extremely sensitive energetic creatures who are constantly receiving and outputting countless bits of sensory data. Every day, and over time, we can accumulate blockages and stagnant energy in our field – most of which is not even ours. Just like brushing your teeth and washing, a basic energetic hygiene practice is essential to maintaining the health of your spiritual being.

When clearing your energy, understand that there are multiple "bodies" or "layers" that make up the individual that is you. We are interacting with reality from each of these bodies, and they each require attention to clear as they affect us on different levels. The 5 body system I work with is: mental, emotional, energetic, spiritual, and physical.

Basic energetic hygiene looks like addressing all these spaces, Do you need to move through the emotional body a little bit with some cathartic release work? Is it deeper-rooted? Is it your actual physical body that needs to be purged?

I always like to start with the subtlest and the easiest to clear, which is the energy field of the space I'm in. There are many clearing agents you can use to cleanse your physical and energetic space. One of my favourite clearing agents is Mapacho, a sacred tobacco plant. I don't inhale it, I just blow it through my energy field, and say a statement of release:

"I now clear myself of any connections outside of myself that are not serving, and I recall my energy and power back into myself."

I don't often work with sage, but many do. Sweetgrass, cedar, and palo santo are other clearing agents. I recommend using plants that are native to the land you're on.

Many people I work with, especially those in the healing fields, need to clear their energy daily in order to show up for their clients at full capacity. Personally, I do regular energetic cleansing every day, and I see practitioners of energetic bodywork and clearing a few times a week.

If an energy has been in your outer fields for long enough without being cleared or addressed, it'll start to penetrate the denser layers of your till it gets close to you. If you're not sub-tly attuned to your field, or if you ignore the signs you get in your intuitive body, you may experience circumstances in your physical body getting to the point where it's something's painful and you have to listen. It actually locks in the physical body, and that's when people get tension and pain.

Try this: Lavender oil on your palms and run your hands from your crown slowly, down your body, with the intention of clearing all 5 of your bodies of any energetic stagnancy and blocks.

Say the following invocation: "I now release any cords and attachments to anything outside of myself and recall all of my power, spirit, and soul back into myself, fully". Repeat this three times and breathe into the body and feel the opening of the top of your head as your energy starts to restore itself. Lavender is a medicine that works on the crown chakra – the centre through which we connect to the divine.

Creating a Connection with the Spirit of Your Business

When you sit at your altar, first clear your own energy field and then clear the altar.

You can use whatever space clearing practice/medicine you desire for this. I personally use tobacco smoke.

If you are using smoke, blow it over all of the parts of your body, with the intention to clear yourself. Then blow it over the altar. You can also use your hands to clear your body and the altar.

Light the candles, then repeat the following (or say something similar):

"I am now open to connecting to the spirit of the medicine of my business.

I call in my spirit guides, ancestors, and the spirit of my business, to guide me to the medicine that wants to weave its way through me and out into the world.

I release anything that is blocking this flow of creative energy now, and from all timelines, dimensions, and realities. I ask that only that which is the highest of good work with me and through me. And so it is."

Allow the silence and space to follow.

During this time, do not try to seek anything, just listen to what is coming into your awareness.

When you are finished, blow out the candles and say, "With gratitude and love, I now close this sacred portal."

It's important to close down your connection with the altar every time, unless you desire to keep the connection open because you want to continue to receive messages from it – I do this when I am writing.

Once you have established this practice and connection with your sacred space, you are ready for the core teaching at the heart of Wild Business™, that will take you deeper into the portal of your vision – the Feminine Frequency Formula™

CHAPTER THREE
The Feminine Frequency Formula™

Now that you've opened the portal to your Wild Business™, it's time to tap into the Feminine Frequency Formula™. I have shared this modality with thousands of people – to help them move emotional blocks and unleash their creative vision with ease.

Having a Wild Business™ means you need to be able to drop into the wilderness that is the body, to move and shift the blocks and obstacles internally, for your business and creative gifts to stream through you easefully.

I don't trust people that I cannot FEEL are in their bodies. Why?

Because there is a disconnect between their hearts and their sex; their feminine.

The feminine is our longing and desire. And unless this part of us is integrated, there will still be a part of us that is following and chasing a false truth. And this cannot be trusted.

Our hearts, our sex, and our bodies are the portal to our deepest most heartfelt yearnings. In order to bring our vision into alignment with our longings and desires for fullness, we need to first be able to hear the tender voice and wisdom of our bodies.

This is why practices that cultivate meditative connection to the body are important. We need to meditate, not just in the conscious realms, but to drop presence into every part of the body and into our flesh. We need deep, sensual, embodied meditation practices, where it is not just about stilling the mind but rather, unlocking the holdings and tensions in the body.

Because we can bring our vision through from the lens of stress or we can bring it through from the lens of pleasure.

And when I say pleasure, I am talking about the ecstasy of truth.

Because sometimes what is in the highest alignment for our soul, will not be pleasurable.

Yes, there is the ecstasy of alignment available to us, but it is usually on the other side of moving through the fear and discomfort of actually committing and showing up for it.

If we are in a state of stress, or fight or flight/survival mode, then our vision will often be the byproduct of this stress. This is where the Feminine Frequency Formula™ comes into play as this is the formula that drops us out of scarcity and into deeper, more receptive feminine states of relaxation.

The Feminine Frequency Formula™ is a practice of feeling through the densities of the body and allowing yourself to drop into a slow, relaxed, theta/beta state of consciousness that I call the darkness. It is a state in which our nervous system feels calm, safe, and receptive.

When you embody this frequency, it creates instant impact in reality. Your words have more potency and power, your actions are more impactful and symbiotic. You naturally become more harmonious and in flow with the world around you.

And, it will also show you any places where you are not living your truth or not aligned with your soul, and those realities will start to purge from your being. I see this in the way prospective clients react to my energy. Even before people actually work with me one-on-one, many experience energetic cleanses, purges, or healings that happen in the days or nights leading up to our first interaction.

With this frequency, you can clear your own energetic blocks, access the full power of your feminine creative force. It is not uncommon for miracles to happen when you start tapping into this frequency.

Everyone who works on my team also creates from this same frequency, which means we're attuned and harmonized at a level that traditional team building models simply can't compete with. There is a psychic field created in our business which makes telepathy second nature.

Creative ideas about the business drop in easily, and each team member is attuned to the essence of the business and movement. This makes the business operate like more of an ecosystem and less of a hierarchy. It is not just one person holding the creative power – all of the team are connected to their own creative power, and have learned how to channel the essence of the brand as I do.

That's the brilliance of the Feminine Frequency Formula™ and how it's led me to create all of my businesses.

It is not about replicating any step-by-step strategy.

It is about shifting into the feminine darkness and the space beyond the mind – where YOU are receiving direct guidance and inspiration from YOUR creative channel.

It will bring through the business that is true for YOU – not a cookie-cutter version of my business or anyone else's.

The Darkness

From a metaphysical standpoint, darkness is the nature of feminine consciousness; it is the void from which life emerges. It is the cosmic womb of creation.

On an energetic level, darkness is a space of receptivity and awareness that lies beneath our surface emotions and beyond all thoughts. It is from this state that I channel all my visions, content, and decisions for my business.

I've found that creating a physically dark, womb-like environment helps me access my creative channel. When I was a kid, my mom and dad and I would often make a drive from our house to Perth, which is four hours away in WA. We drove a Pajero, and there was one seat that was my special seat. I'd make my parents drape and cover the seat with blankets, to create a dark cave for me. I absolutely loved being in there. At home, I'd always be hiding in the kitchen cupboards. I'd put a big soup pot over my head because I preferred to be in the darkness.

Darkness helps us to drop deeper than the mind. Like the depths of the ocean, darkness takes us into the depths of our own self – beyond our thoughts to submerge into our subconscious and beyond.

Darkness is also a key quality of my sacred creation space. I find that it is easier to access the current of my intuition in the dark. Without visual distractions, external stimuli, and too much light – particularly artificial lighting – we can more easily feel into the world beyond our physical senses.

We are constantly receiving sensory input, data, and information from the world of light.

Billboards, ads, and social media feeds populate us with other people's opinions and beliefs on how we should live our lives and run our businesses.

How do we actually distill who to listen to or what actions to take?

It is valuable to receive all of this information from the world of light that we can perceive outside of us.

And it must be balanced with a practice of connecting to the body; to the vessel of sacred creative darkness within us.

The Body Is the Key

A few months ago, I woke up for two mornings in a row with an enormity of pain in my body, particularly in my heart. At that time, I was receiving so many downloads about the next steps I needed to make in my life, which were by no means small decisions – and my body was feeling it.

The pain in my chest grew stronger and stronger until I listened, and responded to what was in my heart. Most people would call this angina and would probably go and be treated, to numb the symptoms and then get back to the very life that's causing them stress in the first place. This is a symptom - reaction - suppression model which is inherent in the way we treat the body in western medicine.

The body streams consciousness.

When we listen to our tension and pain, truth reveals itself to us.

But go one step deeper, learn how to journey the consciousness of the body, and listen to what messages it has for you, and you can consciously evolve through your pain. The Feminine Frequency Formula™ gets us into that space of witnessing our consciousness – instantly.

This is how soul evolution takes place, and how the diamond of our genius imprint is formed.

The truth is, we have all the answers and guidance we need within us.

But in order to have a strong and clear connection with our inner guidance, we have to be willing to face the full spectrum of emotions within us – especially the pain we might not even be aware we are suppressing.

This chapter is an invitation to pause everything you're currently doing in your business, turn off the lights, and go deep into your body.

The Feminine Frequency Formula™ is about slowing down enough so that we can take better action in our business – making quantum shifts into the reality that is aligned with our creative genius.

Quantum Leaps Into Ease

I do so much less now and I'm accomplishing more because I'm connected to this frequency – this feeling, this energy – of the feminine darkness. Being in touch with this place cultivates a sense of deep nervous system relaxation, which allows you to quantum leap out of struggle and force into ease and grace.

The Feminine Frequency Formula™ helps us rewire the parts of our brain that tell us we have to do more. It resets our priorities: to care for ourselves first and make sure that we are feeling good before we take action.

It's counterintuitive to our logical minds that we *can* do less on a physical level and be actually accomplishing more, but it's true. Many people I know don't take out time for themselves, and I know that if they actually did, they'd be more successful. Some believe that surrendering to rest or being in the feminine equals being weak, or that not doing anything equals being lazy.

The Queen within us knows, though, that we achieve more with less effort, once we've prioritized our pleasure, our wellness, and our alignment. She's that one who breathes deep, who eats well, who gets enough sleep.

She knows how to relax.

On some level, we are scared to relax. The minute you relax, all of your trauma around over-doing, forcing, and pushing yourself out of alignment; all the tension you've held in your body from every time you haven't listened to your needs, it all comes up. As soon as we relax, our shadows emerge. We are terrified of facing our demons – the part of ourselves we're not willing to accept. We don't actually *want* to feel our lack of alignment, so after a couple of deep breaths, we go straight back into the old pattern of doing more and covering up our truth.

How long can we deny or repress any part of ourselves without getting sick? The truth is, that all the things we are afraid of feeling are harmless – but avoiding them causes us harm. Built-up tension, trauma and stress weighs on us and throw our entire lives off-balance.

In order to do anything with ease, much less create a business, we have to create a healthy internal environment for ourselves, and this requires facing *all* that we are feeling. The feminine wants you to have Epsom salt baths, long naps, quiet walks in the woods, and all the laughter you can possibly laugh.

She wants you to take slow mornings, put your phone down, stretch your body, and meditate before making moves.

She wants you to create ease for yourself so that it manifests into your business.

A business has many moving parts, and it can be challenging sometimes to maintain this practice. While writing this book, I took a few weeks to attend a training at a mystery school, and it was surprising how long it took me to actually feel fully relaxed in my being, and not like a servant to the energy that tells me I need to do more. However, unlearning these hyper-masculine ways of being is fundamental to the shift that the planet is going through. We don't have to slow to a halt, and we certainly don't have to prevent ourselves from taking action when it feels aligned. But we do have to give ourselves the gift of balancing our action with rest.

I recently had a session with a woman who was so confused about everything happening in her business. She couldn't decide what steps to take and was constantly comparing herself. Our work wasn't about laying out an action plan – it was simply to get her to keep pulling her energy back down and inward to that space of receptivity and listening. Every time she's in that space, there is no confusion.

When we live from this space of deep listening and stillness, anchoring into the core of and the heart of the feminine, there is no confusion, no doubt. All of that dissolves.

There is no secret to this level of clarity and ease – it's simply an energetic shift you make from within the body. I have seen this frequency ignite people's creative gifts and help them easily complete and deliver their projects into the world.

What's amazing is I never actually tell anybody what to do. All I do is emanate this frequency, which bypasses surface level coaching and listens to the unspoken truth of the soul, encouraging whatever is there to come out. Through this frequency, people often tell me that they suddenly feel completely tapped into their core message and what it is that they're here to do. They know what steps to take, and they understand the purpose and intention behind those steps.

The easiest way to tap into the Feminine Frequency Formula™ is through ritual.

Ritual and ceremony are at the heart of the Wild Business™ way. There is nothing dogmatic or religious about this. We use ritual to connect to the spirit world, as much as the material world, as we create across both realms.

Your work is to go on a somatic journey. A feeling journey. To allow and express everything that comes up as you navigate the different layers of emotion in your body, which are the gateways to hearing the voice of your intuition and bringing through your Wild Business™.

The Feminine Frequency Formula™ - The Bridge between Spirituality & Science

The Feminine Frequency Formula is not some woo-woo spiritual ideology not rooted in this reality. It does not advocate for having some transcendental experiences that disconnect you from your body.

In fact, the philosophy of The Feminine Frequency Formula™ is rooted in eight years of scientific research and understanding.

The Feminine Frequency Formula™ works with the nervous system.

It teaches you how to drop into deep parasympathetic states to access what Swiss psychologist Carl Jung once called The Superconsciousness. Some call it God-consciousness and others, the divine. Whatever your reference point, it is the state of consciousness beyond logic, where you can experience the infinite.

On my journey, I have realised this state also correlates with the states of Theta and Delta consciousness – when we slow our frequency right down to these states, we can go beyond logic and access zero-point consciousness. Complete stillness. When we do this, the whispers of the divine become louder and we are granted access to the subtle communication networks that guide us on our soul's path.

How to Tap Into the Feminine Frequency Formula™

Prepare a Playlist

I have created a playlist that I work with, which takes me to the place where I am about to relax and connect deeply with the source of my creative essence and magic.

I suggest that you make a playlist of your own with songs that encourage you to feel deeply. The music you choose acts as an anchor point which can make it easier to connect with this state.

Set and Protect

Enter your sacred space, and set clear boundaries with anyone else you are living with. Ensure you will not be interrupted for the duration of your experience, which will be as long or as short as it needs to be.

Silence distractions, and cut any mental cords of attachment to anyone else's needs or wants of your time or attention.

You can do this by stating: "I now release any ties and attachments to any source of power outside of myself and call my power fully back into my body, now."

Clear your energy field using your personal energetic hygiene practices.

To do this, I burn a light offering of mapacho and trace the smoke around my body and environment, sealing doorways, windows, and energetic portals to the outside world.

When we've done the clearing of our attachments and cleansed our space, then the body will let go into the stillness where we can receive our guidance.

Intend and Allow

Arrive at your altar, and light your candles. Feel your intention to connect with yourself on a deep level, to drop into the body, beyond the mind. It doesn't matter how this looks or sounds – silently, aloud.

What's important is that you are willing to open up to your feeling state.

Breathe.

Notice.

Feel.

Feel and Release

Notice and embrace all the sensations in your body and heart.

Go into them.

Move them through.

Cry.

Dance.

Sing.

Feel.

Breathe some more.

It doesn't matter what thoughts come up, or how your body wants to move. Allow your emotions to be fully felt and released. Gently, slowly, tenderly, fiercely, wildly – whatever your release looks like doesn't matter.

When we have emotional tension and debris in the body, it creates restriction, and we can't drop in any deeper to hear our creative channel.

Your body knows what it needs to release.

Let it all happen.

It is extremely normal to experience a purge of dense energy, emotions, and sensations as you begin to work with this frequency. Sadness, grief, rage, illness, can all come up to be released through this process of feeling intuitively.

Yes, it can literally feel like you're on an Ayahuasca journey.

Don't think about anything while you're in this space. Allow nature to do her thing.

Your breath will calm.

Your brain will relax.

Your heart will open.

Be Still and Know

At a certain point, when you have cleared the denser layers of emotion, you will naturally drop beyond the waves of the surface and find yourself in a space of stillness.

As you feel this, allow yourself to surrender into it.

Lay on your back or settle into a meditation seat. Relax and receive.

Integrate the Experience

Integration is the art of actively choosing to embody the wisdom that you receive from your journey into the dark.

The Feminine Frequency Formula™ initiates deep, cellular reset. In order to get the benefits of this practice, you must give yourself generous time and space to simply do nothing, and be.

Some grounding, integrative practices are writing/journaling, being in nature, swimming and bathing, and preparing a nourishing meal for yourself.

Continue to Deepen

Once you tap into this frequency, you will be amazed at how quickly and easily your business starts to come to life from here.

At the end of the day, the message of the feminine frequency is quite simple: silence distractions, drop into your body and express all the emotions that you can feel in the physical until you are clear and still within. Listen to what emerges from that still point.

This is an act of deep surrender to the current of Nature that is guiding you back into harmony with yourself. This is the way you can birth your creative projects organically, and make decisions with confidence and ease, rooted in a grounded and relaxed nervous system.

As you revisit this space, you will constantly meet new parts of yourself and reveal more of your creative genius.

Your guidance will stream through, and your Wild Business™ will begin to manifest before your very eyes.

CHAPTER FOUR
Landing Your Vision

Now that you've received the Feminine Frequency Formula™, it's time to talk about the practical steps of landing your vision into your reality. A lot of the frustration I feel with people who are starting on this path comes from confusion around what to do with the insights they receive.

Frustration and confusion are gifts – they are indicators that we are in a letting go process, which comes right before our clear channel opens up and we understand exactly what wants to come through us. In this chapter, I'm going to share with you why your emotional experience is key to landing your vision, and how you can recognize the impulse to act on your vision.

Like we talked about in the previous chapter, Wild Business™ is about trusting the mystery and working in partnership with the unseen forces that are collaborating with you to bring about your vision. A big part of this practice is trusting divine timing.

The key to landing your vision is to let go of the time continuum in which you think it needs to happen. If you're forcing it, you're going back into the paradigm which we just awoke from, which keeps you trapped in cycles of struggle and stress.

One thing is true of all visions: they exist on another timeline. The reality we see in our vision is always available to us in the psychic realms, but the physical manifestation of our vision needs time and trust in order to land. Moving the way nature moves, we need to let go of needing to know what's going to be, how, and when.

When we receive a major vision, it's easy to react – to make a decision or take an action from emotion, without truly giving space and time for the vision to land. What we must practice is our capacity to hold the vision, breathe into it, and expand ourselves to become the carriers of it.

The amount of times I've seen it happen: visions being birthed prematurely, actions being taken that weren't quite grounded energetically, choices made from a space of impulse and reaction rather than receptivity and ease...none of this is in harmony with nature.

Like a panther, stalking its prey, hiding in the shadows of the jungle, listening for the most minute changes in the environment, you must receive your vision with sensitivity and awareness, yet hold yourself from pouncing until the moment is just right.

So, what do you do when you're in the space of darkness and you get massive downloads?

1. Once you've received a vision, ask the Universe for anything that's in alignment with the vision to be magnetized towards you.
2. Release this request, and then simply observe what arises in your field as you go on with your life. Be open, investigative, and curious about what you receive.

It is important that when we are communicating with our business, that we do not push or try.

When you are working with manifestation or communicating with the spirit of your business, it is important to hold an intention and then let it go. It is in the moment of letting go of expectations that we actually allow ourselves to receive. When we try, it blocks our receptivity because there is an effort in the system.

The way that I work is to hold an intention in meditation and then to go and do something that takes my mind completely off business. Often my biggest business sales have come through whilst I have been on holidays or doing something that is entirely non business-related. This is because I have opened my body into a state of deep relaxation.

That's not to say do NOTHING.

There are times to move forwards and times to let go. The key is to become a master of both.

Learn how to cultivate deep states of meditative presence and single point awareness where you can assert your desires with your consciousness, into the field of potentiality. And then let it go and be open to how it looks. And when it happens. This is the true power of the feminine.

When the vision wants to land, it'll be driven through the body. You'll feel a response through the body that is like arousal – when something is right and aligned to take action. It arises through your lower centres, your womb, your sex, the seat of the feminine. This is Kundalini energy. That's where she is dormant, and when she awakes, she strikes like a snake. When you feel this energy grounded in your lower centres, that's the opportunity for you to take action. If you miss that window, that can change the whole trajectory of your vision. While there are no mistakes and always more opportunities, it is important to follow the creative impulse when you feel it. When you do, you're adding powerful momentum in the direction of your vision. You are saying "Yes, creative life force, I am listening – move through me and let's make it happen."

A lot of people are fixated on this thought of transcendence, of being able to create from the higher planes, and then ignore the actual physical vessel and the emotional body.

If there are blocked emotions in your body, as soon as you come out of your meditation or your visionary experience, it's like you're back at square one. It's like nothing ever happened. You're still in resistance, you're still in tension. You still feel like you're hitting blocks when you go to make decisions.

Why?

Blocks in your emotional body actually constrict your life force internally, so you don't have a physical experience of freedom through all parts of your being. You're not able to literally feel the creative impulse. You're not relaxed, you're not in pleasure. When there's an emotional block, there's no ease of creation.

If we're creating our business from a place of some kind of unconscious block, things cannot be as abundant, and our business won't provide us with a source of love, inspiration, and joy. Only creating our business from truth brings us this satisfaction. Your business cannot deplete you and it cannot exhaust you when you're connected to that space. But if you're creating something from the space of a block or not from the seat of truth, then it's going to be exhausting.

Often, the emotions we need to process in order to feel this truth are below the surface. We can't just perceive them in our day to day lives; they live deep in our bones and in our past stories.

This is why we have to work with the Feminine Frequency Formula™, accessing the parts of us that are connected to the underworld, below the consciousness. The subconscious and unconscious have their roots in the body, in the emotional body, in our DNA and ancestral lineage.

It is in working with these parts of us that are dense – our matter and our physical being – where we can unlock true freedom as creatives and visionaries.

When we release stuck emotion from our bodies, what is happening is we are letting go of a timeline we've been holding, that we once believed to be true, or that we were once projecting as our possible future. We are creating space for what is alive, here and now.

It is one thing to be able to see a vision; it is another thing to be able to actualize it in the physical. The way that we know if something is right for us or not is by whether we can feel it in our bodies in this physical reality; in matter. The process I walk people through when I am landing their vision is to bring it down from spirit (the heavens) to land in the body (the earth). I support them in clearing any emotional blocks as the vision descends and becomes real, felt, and palpable.

At each level, I ask myself or my client a set of questions and then I use kinesiology and muscle testing to check the blocks at each chakra level, to see what resistance is in the subconscious from the vision fully manifesting at that level. This shamanic journey of descent unravels subconscious layers of information to reveal the truth of the vision.

You can use these questions or ones similar to guide your own visioning process.

For example:

CROWN – What is the higher spiritual purpose of what you are creating?

THIRD EYE – What can you see in your vision?

THROAT – What is your core message?

HEART – Are you open to receiving the vision?

SOLAR PLEXUS – What are your goals? And how will you know when you have achieved them?

SACRAL – Who is your community? Who do you need to get involved?

ROOT – What are your tangible next action steps?

By the end of the process, the vision has landed in their body and they have quantum shifted onto a new timeline where everything is easeful, possible, and achievable.

Tap into Your Inner Child

The feeling of ease in creation is the same feeling of being like a child again. It's an internal sense of freedom and liberation, that when we're connected to it, we also feel externally connected to everything else.

This is the experience of limitless abundance a child has.

They are flexible, adaptable, and can easily reroute their creativity if they are blocked. They can imagine something that we wouldn't even see, and create a normal, everyday experience into a magical adventure.

And if we actually look at children, as soon as there is a block, they fully feel it. They have a tantrum, throw themselves around, and then they get up and it's like it never happened. They carry on creating.

The child carries the spirit of the wild.

This is a key: if we allow our inner child to start to emerge, and we don't try and interpret it or make ourselves wrong about it, then we can keep returning to this state of creativity, aliveness, and innocence.

Innocence is the state of the soul. It's the state where there are no limitations. There are not even any labels. We simply see and experience things from the space of curiosity. When you're in a state of innocence, and when you're connected to the purity of the soul, there aren't mental blocks and mental constructs of right and wrong, or scarcity and lack either. It's not like, "If I choose this thing it means that I don't have that other thing." It's rather, "I'm just curiously going to choose this and see where that takes me."

When you follow those impulses, just out of curiosity, that's when magic can happen. When we have these mental constructs that limit our capacity to see things actually as they are, that's when magic is interrupted, and that's when we hit blocks, and that's what interrupts our capacity to fully create what it is that we desire for ourselves.

It's really about getting out of the head and into the body so that we can use the mind and the head for what they're designed for, which is for us to have precise, creative direction.

The way that I see it is, we've got a lower mental body, which is connected to the throat chakra, and then we've got our higher mental planes and intuition, our third eye and crown, which are our connection to divinity and cosmos, and also our capacity to create with our imagination whatever it is that we desire. This is also where we have our visionary powers. If we want to manifest something, we can intentionally imagine, dream, and create it.

Each of us has a unique soul "blueprint" that carries the true, authentic version of what we're here to create. Practicing the feminine frequency formula invites this soul blueprint to manifest into the world through your body.

When we receive visions that move us, that is our soul blueprint coming online. Sometimes we receive things visually, sometimes we hear words, sometimes we have a felt sense or a deep knowing without any tangible images or sounds.

How do we know whether a vision is truly coming from our soul, from our essence?

Ask yourself:

How do you feel within the creation process?

Do you feel ecstatically alive?

Do you feel clear?

Do you feel like things are flowing easily to you and from you?

If not, there's likely a block somewhere in your energy. It might be something as simple as letting go of the memory of a past lover, or it might be something like moving out of your house, or it might be some kind of block that might not be related to your business at all. You can always use the Feminine Frequency Formula™ to identify and move through whatever is blocking you.

Just like a Zamboni comes on to the ice rink to clear and smooth the ice for a fresh round of skating, this frequency cleanses your energetic "ice rink" to create an inviting environment for your soul to play and your vision to land.

This is how you set yourself up to take action that matters and makes a difference.

Act On It

It doesn't matter how magical you are, if you're not prepared to show up and do the work, your business isn't going anywhere.

As soon as something arises within my field, I respond to it. Nothing is left floating around unlistened to or unchecked.

It's also how you keep momentum in business.

If it's in your awareness, trust it and respond to it.

Because when you leave something days or even weeks, it no longer has the traction and life force behind it, and something newer and more relevant will be there ready to grab your attention.

Here's a challenge for you:

For just one week, action everything you become aware of that you need to do within your business.

Have the uncomfortable conversations instead of looping them in your head.

Make the investment instead of sitting in scarcity.

Aligned action and responsiveness are what create success in business.

CHAPTER FIVE
Feeling Your Feminine Power

When your feminine power comes online, there's no stopping it. She moves like a serpent, like a dragon; fluid, magnificent, and precise. She speaks through dreams and emanates beauty. Her purpose is creation, and she will ignite your passion until you cannot ignore the call to follow it. When you feel your feminine power, life changes. You start to feel turned on, inspired, driven by your desire to create, led by your heart to love more and be of service.

My business started as pure passion; a spark of inspiration and vision. I was driven by an impulse that defied logic. I was a rebel, and I was being shown my calling – to help people ignite their creativity and gifts, to guide them back to the wild in their hearts. The feminine has always been my guiding force, helping me to continually break free of conformity, taboo, and stigma in my own life and carve my path, which has become my contribution to the world.

Now that you have this connection with your body and awareness of how to drop into the darkness, your feminine power can fully unleash. You now know that when blocks arise in your business, they are indicators of stuck emotion in your field that needs to be moved. You are equipped with practices to confidently meet those blocks and quantum jump onto timelines of greater ease. Stay with this process until you're ready. Keep moving your energy through your body.

The awakening of the feminine in the body is a transcendent moment.

I've had many experiences where I've felt this energy awaken in my base and literally take over my spine, like an ecstatic, electric current. When I'm pulsing with this energy, it's like I'm on a medicine journey, and I drop out of physical reality to go within. This pulse is the feminine calling us back into the darkness of the cosmic womb, into the space of what wants to be birthed from inside us.

The feminine is internal, receptive; and the masculine is external, penetrative. She demands us to go into the dark matter of the body – and then beyond that, into the dark energy of the divine feminine. The archetype of Lilith is what I feel in this energy. It's the dark mother, the kundalini serpent that sits within the base of the spine. What's interesting is I do a lot of my work around Lilith activations, and this is the energy that people say to me they experience the most creative awakenings from. I believe this is because the spirit of Lilith connects us to our kundalini energy, our power, and our magnificence.

Many have called her a demon which is not a surprise to me, because she contains the key to feminine darkness and creative power – that which has been demonised for centuries and suppressed, only to be let out behind closed doors.

She is the key and gateway to knowing our shadow and moving beyond it.

And many are petrified of her because she contains our deepest darkest desires, our secrets.

Those that if we admitted to ourselves, would set us free.

I was at the movies once and someone was sitting next to me and was like, "What is that feeling? My whole chair is vibrating." My whole base was vibrating and it was really hard for me to even focus on the movie because when I actually allowed it to move through it took me straight into my creative channel.

Kundalini is dormant in most people, and it can be awakened naturally and intentionally. However, if it can't flow naturally through the body, sometimes a spontaneous catharsis occurs, to clear emotional blocks for us to experience a connection to the divine. I've had experiences being entirely spontaneous in both myself and clients.

As a physiotherapist, I used to have a lot of clients come to me having these experiences of involuntary twitches, cathartic spasms, with no known medical cause. At the time, I had no spiritual background, so I was confused as to why these particular cases kept coming to me. Other practitioners would put it down to psychology, medical scans and it was so interesting because it didn't feel like any other practitioners were receiving these clients. I feel like they always came to me. I saw many cases of conversion syndrome, which basically means that a person had real physical symptoms, but they were attributed to psychological causes of unknown nature because there's nothing detectable in medical scans. I understand why all these clients were coming to me now, because I needed to understand the energetics of what was happening within them. They were having these experiences of kundalini energy trying to move and didn't know how to actually allow it.

One of my personal policies is to stop what I'm doing when I feel stuck and to work with the medicine of shaking or dance. I shake my body and allow tremors and movement to quiver through me.

Alternately I'll go to the medicines of the earth; the beach and the forest, connecting to the ecstatic current of nature.

Instruments like didgeridoo and drum are also incredibly powerful tools for evoking kundalini and allowing it to clear our channel.

When you feel kundalini, move with it. Use whatever medicines of dance, sound, stillness, or touch that you need to allow yourself to receive the benefits of this energy. All it wants to do is clear you out of stuck tension so that you can create more!

People ask me how it is I show up so much and am able to follow through with so many creative projects.

The answer?

I can't hide from my feminine energy. If something wells up inside of me and asks me to feel it, it becomes painful if I don't listen.

I go mad.

Hysteric.

Have you ever wondered what's behind the diagnosis of female "hysteria"... why they call it a hysterectomy when you have your womb removed?

It's this.

A disconnect from the creative seat and essence of a woman – the lack of listening to the wisdom of creation, within the womb. The ancients and indigenous peoples knew how to work with this power but it has been lost in the modern world. Most people are walking around, detached from their power centres, not knowing it exists or not knowing how to summon it to use it in a healthy way. Constantly outsourcing it into others and into the material world.

But when this power stirs and wakes up, you can no longer deny it.

When you're awakened to your feminine power, you realize that Spirit has boundless energy.

Untapped resources. The only thing that stops us from being able to access this unlimited flow of resources is our belief systems – the belief that we are stuck, the belief that we need to heal ourselves first, the belief that we can't... all of it.

When we open our channel and allow this energy to pour through us, everything we need is provided to us. Where people often get stuck is that they forget...

They get locked in old habits that feed the beliefs that they hold.

Create habits that support your feminine flow. My morning ritual is one of the most important parts of my daily routine. I wake up and spend 2 hours in ceremonial space, tuning into the energetics of the day and where I am needing to focus my energy.

I am fortunate enough to have created a life for myself with so much spaciousness to do so and you can, too – have this time for ritual, this time for spaciousness. It comes down to this core ingredient: magic.

Knowing magic means you can command your energy instead of it commanding you.

Your energy has the potential to create and to destroy.

Most people are in cycles of addiction because they don't know how to wield this power.

This is why I did martial arts for years.

It requires a channel.

And this is what kundalini will teach you.

How to have a pristine inner environment for your power and energy to stream effortlessly. As you start to feel shifts in your life and business through the force of your feminine power, don't push anything to happen. Just keep relaxing.

It is important to be aware of where your action is coming from. If you are overexcited, or in fear, or trying to stay safe or comfortable, you're probably not acting from your alignment.

Trust divine timing.

Be wherever you are.

Prioritize your alignment.

The ways that I drop into deeper levels of alignment involve practices that open the body and shift physical tension from my system.

In that state, where I feel then connected to my body, I then just feel into and ask for guidance to come through.

What is it that I need to know about my business?

What is it that I need to do today?

I ask questions and just see what comes through, and then get the answers. That's how I start my day.

Then I let it all go. I go out for a walk or go to the beach. I do far less, and I probably achieve a lot more than a lot of people in a single day, because I'm actioning the most powerfully aligned thing I can within that day.

That's because I've listened. I'm not trying to forge my way forward and make shit happen; I simply listen to what it is I need to do. That might look like contacting two people, who are the ones who end up booking into the program.

Whereas, if I'd gone about my business day from a logical, strategic mindset, making a mental list like, "I need to contact every single one of these people," or "I need to send out this email blast," or, "I need to run more ads," I might not necessarily pull in any clients that day. This kind of action is not actually targeted towards your vision, whereas your intuition is targeted. It's precise. It tells you exactly what you need to do.

If you listen and follow that, you can't go wrong.

PRACTICE: WAKING UP SLOWLY

When we are first waking up, the veils are the thinnest. Is the time when we are most connected to our creative consciousness, intuition, our dreams, and to God.

In the morning, I take my time to get up.

I place my hands on my body and I writhe around and slowly bring sensation into my cells.

I put on some gentle music and I lay there and see if I can recall my dreams.

I utilise this time to ground into my body, to consciously tune in to how I want my day to play out, and how I want to feel. This is the best time to consciously manifest what you want to create for yourself, for the day.

My suggestion is to have half-an-hour to an hour technology-free, and to wake the body up slowly. Gentle movement practices that are meditative, such as yoga or dance, are best before moving into something that elevates the heart rate.

Create space in the morning to have 60-90 minutes to stay in bed. Don't go on your phone for the dopamine hit. Stay in your theta state. This is the best time for manifestation.

To manifest, I drop into deep stillness and I ask, "What wants to reveal itself to me today in relation to _____?" So, for example, if I am wanting clarity on what to do in my business, I specify that.

I don't always receive instant answers, however, if the seed and the question are planted, the answer always comes. You just need to be open to how it reveals itself to you.

The other day, for example, I was thinking about selling one of my businesses, as I had started to lose drive and the desire to run multiple businesses and decided I just wanted to focus my energy into the one.

I did a tantric self-pleasure practice and was meditating during the practice, dropping into deep stillness and asking which would be in my highest and best interest to sell.

Immediately after the practice, I received a phone call with an issue in one of the businesses – a client was complaining about a service and I immediately knew, that was the business I needed to sell.

This is what I mean when I say that the answers don't always come in the way we EXPECT them to come.

God did not just show me a vision of one business being sold. I received a tangible manifestation and confirmation as soon as I completed my practice and was moving back into my regular day.

Once we have an intention to know something, we then need to let it go entirely.

The answer always gets delivered.

We just need to be open to hearing the messages.

Now, you've opened the vortex of unlimited possibilities. You're tapped into the infinite nature of reality, where you have all the creative potential of the Universe in your hands.

This is where many people take on the identity of, "I can't do this."

Don't fall into this trap and get overwhelmed.

Your feminine power asks you to be still and slow. She wants you to take your time, to relax, to indulge in every moment, to romance the mystery.

CHAPTER SIX
Business is Sex

How you do sex is how you do business. This is why I believe that having a conscious sexuality practice, one that helps you to experience the ecstasy of slowness, is so important for keeping your business aligned. It actually feeds into and translates into more presence and beauty in all areas of your life.

Feminine sexuality has long been repressed and demonized by the patriarchy, but the truth of the matter is our sexuality contains all the pure potential energy that we need to build, lead, and create. When our sexuality is repressed, blocks, illness, and stagnation can manifest in our business. When our sexuality is flowing and expressed, we're healthy. Just like in romantic relationships, the way you relate with your business sets the tone for the quality, depth, and excitement you will experience. I want to share with you some basic tantric principles and practices that I use every day to integrate and work with my sexual energy so that my life and business keep flowing.

Have you ever felt into your body while you are creatively inspired? When a big surge of creative energy moves through you, do you feel your body being turned on?

Within all of us lies an energy so strong that it can create life as we know it. This force lives deep within our primal roots; our womb (or cosmic womb), our sex centre, and our hips. Our sexual energy is what inspires us to reach out to people, to share our expression, to make deep connections with clients, channel copy and create content. When we allow this taproot to nourish us, running upwards to the higher centres of our heart and mind, we can create anything we desire.

Understanding that you have unlimited access to creative energy is one thing, but knowing how to unleash it is another. We crave a fertile life experience, and when we feel ourselves cutting off our sexual life force just to be in the sterile world of corporations, it's like a slow drip poison. On top of this, a lot of us need repatterning around what sex actually is. There's a collective sense of rush, obligation, pressure, responsibility, and performance around the sexual experience that has run rampant in our society. People treat it as an act to get themselves or their partner off. If they don't orgasm, they feel like something is wrong; like they have failed.

I worked as a Red Tantra practitioner for a few years, in Melbourne, giving men Tantric teachings to support them to experience something deeper than what they receive in surface-level reality – a connection with their own body and sexuality that touches their divine nature and gave them a remembering of what it is to experience heaven on earth.

This place that is heaven on Earth exists as an internal state of being, to be cultivated with the practices I speak about in this book and teach in my trainings. It's about taking the shame and stigma out of our normal, natural feelings.

You can work with your animal body, sexual desire, and primal instincts to allow them to become a source of something that fuels your spirit. You can transmute raw sex, power, and emotions so that you can experience something more fulfilling and longer lasting in your connections.

With the work that I teach, I've been called the devil and portrayed as evil by all kinds of people who still link sexuality – and the feminine – to something sinful, dangerous, and taboo.

If we look at the origin of some of this conditioning around sexuality, we see that a lot of it comes from the institution of religion. God (the masculine; consciousness) is preferenced over Goddess (our sensuality, emotional nature, compassion, intuition, and desire). There is also a split between spirit and sex, with sex being denied as evil – and look how far it that has gotten us from our true nature.

The feminine is our gateway to freedom. She destroys anything that's not real and alive and it's not truth. When she's activated, she can't tolerate bullshit, lies, and control, and the church is about control. So if she unleashes, it would all collapse, which is what we saw in real-time when the Notre Dame Cathedral burned in Paris. That happened on a really major astrological date, a really powerful alignment where two archetypal feminine Goddesses, Venus and Lilith, met in the skies at the 23-degree mark of Pisces in aspect to Pluto (the planet associated with the dark goddess and the shadow; the energy of death and destruction) at 23 degrees, right after Eris in Aries was conjoined with the sun at 23 degrees- a Cardinal Grand Cross. Lilith represents the dark feminine centre, and she destroys illusions. Venus representative of beauty and

Eris, the goddess of chaos, strife, and discord, in the fiery sign of Aries, conjunct the sun, the burning. Notre Dame means "our lady" and I believe that this is all divine symbolism, as the feminine cannot be controlled.

You can't live an illusory life when the feminine is at play. When your sexual current is flowing through you, nothing false can take control of you.

She tears that shit down.

You'll feel it.

When you have attuned your own nervous system to slowness, anything that's loud and abruptive to the nervous system becomes fragmenting to our system, and then it becomes intolerable. And that's how we come back to moving from intuition, because something that's not of resonance actually hits a pain point, creates suffering, and then guides us back to the place of feeling connected to self.

In my own life, learning Tantra has been the gateway to learning how to slow things down in my sexual life. The more I practice ecstatic slowness in the bedroom, the more it shows up in my work. I feel more pleasure, ease, subtlety, and magnetism in my business. I have infinite energy to do what needs to be done. And I feel like I'm honouring myself every step of the way; not cutting corners or compromising what my body needs.

When my sexual energy becomes stagnant or blocked, my business usually stops flowing. Tension in our system gets stored in our lower energy centres – within our root and sacral chakras. Our creative, emotional, and sexual energy are synonymous. We know that we have repressed energy in these spaces if we are not naturally inspired and our creative energy is not flowing through us organically.

The key to opening up to deep creative states is by shifting the blocks within our creative energy centre and replenishing our Jing (the sacred elixir of life, stored within our sacral centre). One of the most beautiful and natural ways to awaken this energy is through a regular pleasure practice that combines breathwork, meditation, and a tantric self-pleasure ritual, in one. Tantric practices help us break down the internalised patriarchal structures which tell us we have to leave our longings at the door, in pursuit of a business that controls and restricts our creativity.

Tantric practices for deep ecstatic slowness

Yin Yoga

One way to keep the primal energy centres unlocked, is through a deep yin yoga practice daily, to keep flexibility through the hips and in particular the psoas, which is the muscle that contracts when we have suppressed sexual, emotional, or creative energy. Poses such as butterfly, reclined butterfly, happy baby, swan, and dragon pose are all great hip opening postures that can free up stored primal energy.

Sounding

Sound is also a really powerful way to liberate and free the body of stuck energy – try working with gibberish – allowing yourself to make any noises that come out of your mouth. Let go of how they sound and just allow the sound to come out as it desires to.

Breath

Your breath is the barometer that shows you what's happening in your mind. It's like the first instance of stress in the body, the breath is the first thing to re reflect that. Change your breath and slow it down and it slows your nervous system down. When we slow down, we become more present and we feel more. The breath is the ultimate gateway to sexual and personal liberation.

Touch

Lovingly touching your own body stimulates healing and growth in your cells, revitalizes your energy, and connects you with your soul. My personal practice of touch looks different every day and is totally contingent on what my body needs. Listen to your body and give yourself the touch it craves.

Slowness

When we slow down, we feel more.
Slow down. Feel more.

Presence

Simply creating the space to be fully present with yourself and your sexuality can open up a world of miracles. As we learned with the Feminine Frequency Formula™, there are many layers to the emotions that can come up as we dive into the body. Be present with yourself as you would with a lover; honour your heart and let yourself feel.

Personally, I have a daily practice that combines all these elements. I use it to slow my nervous system right down, to move and circulate my life force for greater vitality.

A lot of people are open to the idea of Tantric practice but have resistance to dropping into this level of self-pleasure and slowness. This is because these practices help you to regulate your nervous system, and therefore anything that's out of alignment becomes loud. And people don't want to hear what's hidden beneath the surface, because they don't want to let go of their stress patterns.

Slow sensuality practices are a gateway to our deepest knowing and also, to our shadows – the parts we don't want to hear, see, or validate out of fear of having to change our preconditioned ways. When we start intentionally working with our sexual energy, we start to experience our shadow, and many people will back away. But if you want to have a successful business, you also have to be willing to look at your shadows and you have to be willing to show up for the things that are uncomfortable in your life. Sexuality is the greatest teacher of this.

We can't know truth unless we allow ourselves to feel what's aligned and what's not, and the feminine feels, and so by shutting her down – repressing our sexuality – we create an easy, safe identity to hide behind so we can keep living our lies.

It's a choice we have to make. Our sexual experiences can be yet another act of hiding our wild – of pretending, of faking orgasms and connection, of covering up our true desires and heart – or, they can be an unravelling back home to our truth, if we are willing to surrender control and to allow ourselves to be taken by the ecstatic rapture of feeling. Deep sexual intimacy is one of the most vulnerable, beautiful, and courageous experiences we can have as human beings. When we truly open up our sexual energy during intimacy, there is no hiding. We are raw, naked, open, and have the ability to surrender into our deepest longings, emotions AND also, insecurities.

The gateway to truth is through feeling.

The same goes for business.

Many people are able to show up for jobs and "work" every day, bearing and grinning it and pretending everything is okay – no real vulnerability, honesty, and transparency about what is really happening underneath the mind's facade.

You can show up to something you don't like every day by locking your consciousness off from your body. You can listen and create a symbiotic relationship with your business and its desires of where it is wanting to go, or you can try to control it out of the desire to have things go the way you want them to.

This is why there are so many health issues in society because people are ignoring their truth. They have separated themselves from their deeper longings and desires, represented by the body; the feminine. If you practiced running this energy through your body, it would waken and clear your emotional body. You'd have to feel. And perhaps you would feel grief in your heart, at living a life in an existence that you hated, maybe being in a relationship you feel trapped in. Your whole reality could break down because once you truly acknowledge that you can't continue feeling a certain level of pain, reality has to shift.

It's so important to feel these things because, eventually, you will get to a point where you cannot stand the pain of lying to that part of yourself. I've seen this pain manifest in women as menstrual and reproductive issues. Our womb space is where we hold and carry our emotional energy, our sexual fire, and our creative power, and when it's clogged up with unprocessed trauma and unfelt pain, we can manifest experiences of disease.

I've seen these same women who come through my training have miraculous healings around their reproductive issues; within a few days of attuning to the energy of the feminine, she clears the blocks and allows natural healing to resume.

I once had a client come to me with chronic low back pain and endometriosis. We did a 1:1 session together and I tuned into her body and could feel a deep trauma being held in her pelvic floor. I did an energetic clearing session and prescribed her a practice using a black obsidian yoni egg – an Ancient Taoist practice, used for restoring sexual energy and Jing to heal and replenish a woman's vitality. During the healing, she experienced deep sexual trauma from when she was a child re-emerge. There was repressed rage being stored through her pelvic bowl, which she released with the session and yoni egg work. Since then, she has been well, with no on-going symptoms of pain or issues with her cycles and womb.

And yes, it can be this simple.

My work is not about simply tracking physical symptoms. It clears them from their roots. This means, in many cases, returning to a pain-free existence. But remember, when it comes to truth and listening to your body, this is a long-term commitment – a life-long practice.

As you already know, you and your business are in a relationship.

When you commit to your business, you're committing to an evolving partnership that will challenge you. Your business will bring out the best in you, and it will also show you parts of yourself that you may not necessarily want to see. Your business can be wildly alive, sexy, and ecstatic. It can flirt with you, tease you, arouse you, and entice you...it's all about how much you choose to lean into that experience.

When we connect with our desire and apply our sexual energy and life force towards our business calling, we create a whole new vibration for ourselves when it comes to showing up for our work. We start to integrate the experience of plea-sure and truth into every phone call we make. We experience a level of impact and influence that is deeper and more satis-fying than simply making sales or completing a contract.

When we embrace our sexuality and slow it down with Tantric practices:

We charge up our auric field with possibility, prosperity, and success.

We tell the Universe that we are in a receptive mode, and start to attract what we desire at an even faster rate.

Our bodies and nervous systems relax into a parasympathetic state of stability and ease.

We are more in touch with what feels good, and what does not. Our intuition sharpens.

If you're starting on this journey and feeling like you're coming up against fears, keep leaning gently into them, like you would with a lover. Remember that just like in any relationship, passion can burn you out. Going hot, heavy, and fast all the time will lead to stress. And doing anything that doesn't genuinely feel good will cause you pain.

Be easier on yourself.

Focus on stabilizing your nervous system.

Listen deeper.

The slower the sex, the deeper you drop, the more you unlock through your subconscious.

This is the recipe for intuition that is on fire – crystal clear and on point.

And it's the key to a business that is dripping with passion and purpose.

CHAPTER SEVEN
Knowing Your Path

"Your business always changes," she said. "You triggered me into realizing that I don't give myself permission to listen to myself or change directions in my business. You just give yourself permission... you don't wait."

This was a conversation I had with a business leader recently, who told me she was triggered about how I was always changing what I was creating in my business.

But, here's the thing...

Adaptability is my superpower – and it can be yours, too.

My ability to trust the mystery of life, and adapt accordingly, has been what's created my success. I read the field, sense into the direction of the current and what's needing to be done, and engage my capacity to radically listen and respond to that. This is the power of intuition.

It seems like a paradox to do business from an intuitive place. Isn't business supposed to be routine, regimented, reliable? Intuition is spontaneous, unpredictable – sometimes chaotic.

We never know what will arise from the depths of our consciousness when we tap in.

We don't know anything at all, actually.

But isn't that kind of comforting?

Isn't it nice to know that we don't have to know anything?

The foundation to building a sustainable business is trusting our intuition over anything else. Many of us have deep-seated blocks to trusting – trusting ourselves, trusting our guidance, trusting other people – because our sense of safety was compromised in some way throughout our earlier years, or on other timelines.

We are all born with a unique soul, a path, and a vision that is only for us. This path is always revealing itself to us through our feelings. We are always given opportunities to hop on and cruise downstream with the flow of creation.

Your path unfolds in miraculous ways. It cannot be planned, controlled, or predetermined in any way by human means. It can only be sensed, felt into, and embraced from an open heart and mind that are willing to bend and adapt to the current of life.

Knowing your path is about committing to moving through all the emotions that block you from feeling safe and secure with the mystery of the unknown.

It's also about utilizing the many blueprints available to you to help you discover your unique gifts and understand your life path. Some of my favourite blueprints to work with are Western astrology and the Gene Keys by Richard Rudd.

We have a great choice in who we want to be, moment by moment... but there's just no denying that we have an energetic map laid out for us that DOES govern and steer our individual human behaviours. Deny the stars and you deny nature.

And as J.P. Morgan once said, "Millionaires don't use astrology, Billionaires do."

Knowing your soul map is smart. Letting it rule you is not. The twist is that I use those blueprints to help people break free of the blueprints.

You can use these maps to identify core archetypal patterns in your soul and awaken new understandings of why you behave, think, feel, and create the way you do.

Together, this powerful combination of intuition and insight can help you intentionally create the life you want.

We can continue to perpetuate all kinds of stories around why it's hard for us to trust life – and ourselves. Or, we can choose to create more trust, by dropping in to our intuition regularly and listening to it deeply. This is the only way we can truly receive the sense of safety and stability we seek from the outside world.

When we're creating from this space of empowered self-understanding, our sense of self-worth and confidence is innately higher – we know we're on the right track.

It's easy to get distracted if we waste time comparing our paths to others. The truth is, you, your genius, and your life cannot be replicated. Often, an idea will land in the collective field and many people will receive it. Seemingly spontaneous mass trends and memes show us that our ideas and imaginations are connected in the nonphysical.

So how do you know if an idea is for you?

The simple answer is, you will feel it resonating in your body at all levels. There won't be a doubt in your heart that you are in alignment. It will feel easy, right, effortless, and true at the core of your being. Anything that's not coming from your true genius essence is going to be hard work.

In order to be on your path and effortlessly manifest your vision, you have to follow what your intuition tells you to do – even if it asks you to enter the crucible of inner purification.

THE BIRTHING OF WILD GRACE

It was the 30th of September 2018, 3:30 in the morning. I had just started my menstrual bleed. To me, bleeding is a magical period of deep rest where I get to descend into the womb of creation, cleanse and release the month's cycle, ready to rebirth vitality back into my body and reset my creative direction. It is when my intuition is at its strongest. On this particular night, I woke up to the song "20 minutes" by Carbon Lifeforms turning itself on through my headphones. As the song started playing I simultaneously started streaming through a vision.

I saw myself teaching around the world. I saw women on stages performing wild, erotic, emotive dance and expressive, very primal.

I had had the name "WILD GRACE" come through for me years before – I had created a website and workshop content, but it never quite felt right.

When this vision landed, I knew immediately that this was what the name WILD GRACE was for.

When I surrendered to the vision and asked spirit about my next moves, I heard, "You need to create a film, capture this visually for people." And so I did that. When I put the video up, I was flooded with messages from people saying essential-ly, "Whatever that is, I need that."

From that space, I started birthing workshops and events, and they were filling constantly because people could feel the energy behind what I was creating.

I was taken by something that was far greater than my-self. Moved by the vision.

I had no choice but to surrender.

I never planned for what I was creating to be a teach-er training that would scale and serve thousands of women from around the world. I simply followed the impulse that came through me.

If there is ever a moment in time where I am THINKING about how to make something work, I know that I haven't sur-rendered deeply enough for the idea to come TO me.

Because here is the thing: you are not the thinker. This is a principle taught by many different Ancient philosophers, from Buddhism to the Vedanta. We are not the ones that come up with our thoughts. We have receptors, like a TV antenna that picks up on frequencies and vibrations, that come through to us as though they are thoughts.

The more sensitive and receptive we are, the more we receive. There is an abundance of thoughts available to be streamed through us. But the ones that are meant for you will not simply be ideas. They will arrive as a feeling that moves you. As a wave of ecstasy through your whole body.

These physical indicators are not reserved for the highly gifted. They are natural and will flow regularly once you're in a consistent practice of tuning in. Pretty soon, you'll notice your intuition overrides any type of logical effort you can put in. I once sat down to "work out" a strategy that took half an hour, to get me to the place I already had seen in a vision, in an instant. So I don't bother with "working things out" anymore. It only ever gets me to the same place I knew and felt I would end up all along. By the time you tried to THINK of the strategy, you could have already have been on the direct route to creating what it is you were trying to think your way to becoming.

Another time, I sat with my accountant and was calculating the budget. I had already had a number come to me – the number of clients I felt I wanted, and the income I needed to generate that month to support my budget. We spent half an hour in calculation and ended up coming back to the same numbers I had already seen and felt come through for me intuitively. I've also hired people to help me with strategy in the past, and it has boxed my intuition in and blocked the flow of organic growth in my business.

The reason why I am a huge advocate for working with the Feminine Frequency Formula™ and having regular embodiment practices to move through the stagnancy and emotional blocks of the body is because when our channel is open, our action comes as a force of inspiration, like lightning, that naturally moves us forwards in the direction of our vision.

There is little thought involved. A higher power works through you.

This means that you manifest the vision with little "hustle" and push. Because wherever you are hustling and pushing, you are not trusting your path.

You are not trusting the ecstatic current of the feminine that already knows the best moves forwards.

She is your intuition.

And if you listen to and follow her, she is the direct route and pathway to manifesting and creating your vision.

You don't need strategy.

You don't need to sit down and plan content.

The content streams through you.

Three Ways to Liberate Your Creative Energy

The next time you are feeling creatively blocked or needing to move some emotional energy in order to get in touch with your intuition, try one of these easy embodiment practices:

SHAKING

Often the simplest and quickest way to move energy out the body. Don't think about it, just let your body shake. Head to toe, as wild or as subtle as you need, for as long as you need. Bonus if you allow yourself to vocalize and make sounds – grunt, holler, yell, wail, chant, moan, laugh – have a blast.

HITTING PILLOWS

Going to war with your bedding is a peaceful and non-destructive way to unleash your emotions. Grab your pillows and hit them. Stomp on them, punch them, shake them, throw them (safely), and then hit them again. Then perhaps build a fort, or have a cuddle with yourself. Let your inner child feel safe and at rest.

FREEZE & RELEASE

If you're feeling a lot of nervous energy or tension, try this: allow yourself to freeze. Completely. Take a breath in, take all the energy you're feeling, and contract completely into yourself. Squeeze tight. Suspend your breath. Freeze time. Observe.

Then release – exhale, loosen, shake, move, and repeat.

Do this until you feel a sense of relief.

These practices soothe the primal, animal, and child energy within us and help us get clarity on our path. We can't experience the magical flow of abundance that wants to come into our business if we're constantly ignoring what our intuition tells us.

When we are consistently in a practice of listening to our intuition and liberating our emotional energy, our path is clear. We turn on our full magnetic power – and that's when magic starts to happen in our business.

CHAPTER EIGHT
Magnetism: Where Magic Happens

Magnetism is nature's marketing model. Like a spider, who weaves her web with chemicals that naturally magnetize her prey, our sexual energy, when turned on, activated, and alive, naturally draws to us everything that is aligned to our vision.

My marketing method is intuitive.

It is organic.

It does not work with manipulation or sales "tactics".

It is honest (sometimes brutally so) and people are drawn to my truth.

"I just need to work with you... I don't know why... I don't even know what it is that you do – but I know I need to work with you."

This is what more than 50% of my clients tell me when they start working with me.

My branding, marketing, and messaging are channeled through ritual processes and are directly connected to my essence.

I still believe traditional marketing tactics, like building out funnels and advertising campaigns can work. I just don't believe that they can be both sustainable and fulfilling if they don't first serve the essence of a business.

Connecting to the essence of your business and opening the communication lines with the spirit of the business need to come first. Marketing tactics amplify that energy. This is where people get stuck. They think that if they have the logistics and the formula in place, that their business will thrive.

It won't.

The key is getting the *energy* behind the message clear and making sure the business is thriving, vital, and that you are feeling connected and inspired by its message and core values/philosophy/offerings.

So what about strategy, then?

As I've mentioned in previous chapters, the type of strategy that happens when we work with our intuition is very organic. Things may appear to be random, but they are part of a higher organized plan.

When it comes to practical matters like naming and pricing programs. It is through working with the Feminine Frequency Formula™ that I am always able to receive guidance on what my offers need to be called, what price point feels like the right amount. From there onwards, I trust. I engage my creative team, I put the offering out on my platforms, and I drop back into a state of continual listening to find out where the offering is wanting to be promoted and to whom. Every time I have attempted to work with more traditional marketing methods to launch and fill a program, I have had fewer clients book in.

I believe the anchoring in of feminine creation is about allowing our natural magnetism to do its thing.

As a child, one of my favorite things to do was to go fishing with Dad. I was a fish whisperer; it was always such a magical experience.

We'd go out on the boat, and I would communicate telepathically with the fish. I would literally pull up one after the other. No one on the boat would be catching anything, but they'd watch me and marvel. "It's the fish whisperer, she's at it again!" I didn't even know I was doing magic then.

From my experience, it was as if I had this sonar radar, of being able to see and feel where the fish were. And I just pulled them through.

The way that I've birthed businesses and launched offerings has always been like this: a psychic, intuitive experience or feeling.

I have attempted to bring in people into my business to work with marketing methods that have ended up losing me clients.

Why?

They didn't get IT.

They were stuck in the formulas, trying to figure out how to bring the clients in.

Because what works for marketing large scale, masculine-minded corporations is not going to work for a business that is feminine led. All systems and structures need to support the vision that is ALREADY within you, not the other way around.

You don't think your way to your clients.

You feel yourself.

And they feel you radiating your authenticity within your business.

This is the major change we are seeing in business at the moment.

People can naturally feel when you're in that state of deep self-connection when you're creating, and they become willing to pay you. Aligned and connected feminine energy is very attractive to people. When we're moving from that space and exuding our divine authority, marketing becomes unnecessary and sales become a byproduct of us putting our creativity out into the world.

Something about entrepreneurs I've worked with is noticing that they just get turned off about the whole idea of marketing, thinking that there's something wrong with them, because they can't write copy, or they can't do sales, and they think it's like some kind of deficiency that they have. It's not just that they hate the model. It's like they feel like they can't even do it.

There's a lot of business advice that says, "If you're not doing it this way, then there is something wrong with you. You need to move past that."

No, actually; the block is valid.

Let's look at how we can use the block to guide us back to something that feels more aligned and useful for you.

If you feel resistance to marketing, strategy, and sales, it may be that you don't have a resistance to those things. You might actually just have a resistance to how they have traditionally been done. This resistance is a positive indicator that you're aligned with something deeper. Traditional methods are not connected to essence; they're coming from the logical mind. Sales are based on numbers and conversion. There's a disconnection to the humanity of the 1-1 interaction, disconnection from the heart.

Attracting aligned clients can only come from this embodied space of the wild feminine. When you're hustling to get clients or sell a program, it becomes easy to compromise on the quality of people you're working with. I used to feel like clients were taking from me, and that's because the clients I was attracting were reflecting to me the parts of myself that I needed to upgrade. They were showing me where I was still giving away my time and energy in a way that didn't serve my highest alignment and values. I was not acting as the Queen that I am; I wasn't feeling her or emitting her frequency.

Whenever I am not attracting clients that I absolutely adore working with, it is because I am not in my creative genius; I am not wearing my divine crown.

It is never really about the other person.

It is always about my own relationship with myself.

The same goes for you.

If the clients that walk through your door are not bringing you joy to serve, it is because you are still not aligned with your highest genius potential. The Feminine Frequency Formula™ and the practices that I teach in my workshops and training align you to your genius in an instant.

This results in your ideal clients naturally being magnetised to work with you.

Modern and mainstream marketing methods are based upon control methods. They are based upon "hooking" clients.

Even the word hook has the energy of manipulation intertwined into it.

When you create a business from beyond the logical mind, through communication with the divine, logical concepts become irrelevant. It becomes less about your target market and how to "hook" clients and more about simply following the potency of energy and trusting that by doing so, everything that is meant to unfold will – but, it is beyond your control.

Because when your business is vibrating with intention and holds its potency of frequency, there is no "hooking" involved. People simply feel the energy behind it and that becomes your marketing method.

Your channel and its vibrational quality send ripples through the cosmos which is palpably felt by the people that need to receive it.

I have a practice where I sit at my business altar, anchor my energy into the core of the earth, and send out vibrational signals, like a sonar, through the mycelium network of the earth. I then speak that I am intending on everyone that needs the medicine I am holding to feel and come into contact with my work and be effortlessly drawn to what I am creating.

And then I let it go.

From that space, I respond to what comes into my field – the ideas, the people I need to contact.

There is no effort or doing, and when I am taking action on anything it is in response to the higher guidance I am receiving, and so it is effortless, pleasurable, and natural.

Probably the most interesting result of working this way is that I regularly get messages from people saying that I've visited them in their dreams and that they've gotten clear guidance to work with me. It happens so often that it's become somewhat of a natural screening process – I know that the people who are receiving my essence in dreamtime are running on the same current as I am, and will likely be aligned clients for me.

I'd like to share with you a dreamtime medicine ritual that you can practice to enhance this power in your own life.

DREAMTIME MEDICINE RITUAL

It is during our sleep that our consciousness state purifies itself.

Scientifically, what happens when we drop into deep meditative and sleep states is that the glial cells around our nerves contract and the toxins that are in our nervous system have the opportunity to leach out and be filtered back into the circulatory system to be excreted.

If we do not get deep rest, this process does not happen and will result in us waking up "tired" or foggy minded. It is in our sleep state that we replenish, and this is important in order to remain clear and connected to our intuition.

The dream state is an important entrance point into the subconscious realms.

Yes, it is possible to bridge dream states and waking states, but for the most part, what is hidden and harder to access during waking state comes through in our dream state as our brain waves drop into deeper states of consciousness.

When working with any conscious or lucid dream practices, there are a few important steps to consider.

Your dream state is the time that you are the most open and vulnerable, and if you are going to be opening yourself to receive communication your dream state, you want to ensure that the information that you are bringing in is accurate and not filtered through the lens of having an unclear astral (psychic) field.

To do this, a purification statement or intent at the start of your dream practice is important.

Below is the practice I do before bed every night.

1. I have an Epsom salt + magnesium bath
2. I clear my energy field with tobacco. I then rub therapeutic grade lavender oil into the palms of my hands, inhale it deeply and take my hands over the crown of my hand and sweep them over my body, slowly.
3. I invite plants and minerals into my space. I place a sachet of salt under my pillow to purify my field while I sleep. Next to my bed, I place deep purple flowers that carry the frequency of high magic and alchemy – morning glory, blue lotus, and datura.

4. I often work with plant tinctures such as mugwort, Calea, or blue lotus to activate a lucid dreaming state.

5. I state my intention, using words such as, "My intention for my dream state is to learn more about _____. I ask that only the purest, highest wisdom and guidance be permitted into my dream state."

6. Optional: I play my sacred playlist to encourage an easeful drop-in to the dream state.

7. I allow space in the morning to remember my dreams.

When you are first waking up, you are still in a state of lucidity where it is possible to remember your dreams. In the mornings, I make sure that I wake up in a relaxed state and I lay in bed for half an hour, recalling my dreams through a process of meditation.

Take this opportunity in the morning to record any insights that you received overnight. Sometimes insights will trickle or pop into your awareness later in the day.

This dreamtime ritual is simply an example that you can modify.

Keep this practice up and you will start to amplify your natural magnetism in magical ways.

CHAPTER NINE
Embodying Your Wild

Embodying your Wild Business™ means living your dream life: switched on, turned on, and abundant. You are calling in co-creators, clients, and partners at even higher levels, who see you and understand your vision. Embodying your wild means surrendering the idea that you have to do it alone.

You share yourself, and you're received by people who are drawn by your essence and your energy.

Your work is feeding you.

It's feeding others.

Your instinct to give, to serve, and to help others grows.

You start to attract clients and co-creators at even higher levels.

Your relationships thrive. Your money spiral goes up.

With all the practices you've learned in this book, you're fully equipped to lead from the seat of your feminine power and your artistry.

Your life and your business are one. There is no separation. No drain. No pressure.

Life brings you pleasure again. You're finding more time to appreciate and savour existence. Surprises and delights become a regular occasion in your reality. Even though there are challenges and dips on the journey, your flow and momentum from this space are unstoppable.

This is the feminine: relaxed, sensual, empowered, confident, and alive. She is deeply in tune with the people around her and the environment around her. She's excited knowing that her day is full of opportunities to connect with her web and grow. She knows that prioritizing the connections that come to her intuitively is always going to yield magic.

We can only know this true space of embodying the feminine once we've undone everything that is not that. A lot of women come to my training with fertility or menstrual cycle issues and will have miraculous healings as we work together. These reproductive issues are largely systemically rooted; it's as if our bodies are resistant to bringing children into these environments where our own feminine health and wellbeing are dismissed. As the old ways of doing business are dying, these new ways that are emerging are showing us that we've always known what to do; how to raise our children, how to take care of the earth, and how to create change in our communities.

Patterns of conditioning and fear will continue to come up as we – and our businesses – continue to evolve. On this path, we are forever promised the experience of birth, growth, and death of identities that no longer serve us.

The key here is to maintain a strong connection to your heart. The heart is where the feminine rests. She is the voice of unconditional love, after all; and she desires a win-win-win outcome. When it comes to being a boss, running a team, and working with others, the core of the heart is our strongest ally.

We must embody the fertile, life-giving, maternal nature of the divine feminine whilst we give direction and make decisions.

When we're deeply connected to the core of our hearts, we have a sense of affirmation that tells us we are already enough. When we share this sense of affirmation with our teams and our clients, we create a nourishing environment for our business to grow. But if that voice isn't there, then our work is really in reconnecting to it.

There have definitely been times when I've been so busy that I've completely lost my connection to that voice. Therefore my actions have sometimes come from a place of feeling like I need to do more in order to be something or to receive love. The heart already knows that we're inherently worthy, loved, and loveable.

The heart is also a paradox. It's both intricate and simple, delicate and fragile, and the most fucking powerful thing in the world. It can function on its own without us doing anything. It has its own electromagnetic circuit. It generates its own pulse.

Embodying our wild means tuning in to our hearts over our minds.

Our heart is the gateway to synchronicity. It's the thing that electromagnetically pulls us towards what we're wanting.

This morning, I didn't feel clear about what to do. I didn't have any particular direction or impulse towards my business. I could have sat there and thought about it, tried to map out a strategy, or made a list. But I would have gotten nowhere. So I told myself, "I'm just going to go and drive until I know what to do."

I was in the car, and all of a sudden, I felt the impulse to go to a certain café.

Now, I had a friend in town who'd wanted to meet up with me earlier in the week. I'd told him I couldn't catch up with him because I wanted to keep my week open and give myself space to rest.

Lo and behold, who do you think was at the café I intuitively visited?

My friend and I meeting happened organically; I didn't need to figure anything out. I didn't need to make plans. When you're connected to your intuition and living from your heart, you don't need to make plans. You don't need to figure anything out, and all that needs to happen happens anyway. You just have to keep moving, and following the tug of the heart and where it shows you to go.

Everything self-organizes when you're connected to your heart. You don't have to create these massive organizational structures. I hired someone recently to do that, and a day in, I was like, "I can't do this." Everything in my business works perfectly without an org chart, and it's not how I work. I just needed to finally admit that to myself.

Really, there are no limits to what you can achieve when you reach this level of embodiment. In fact, it's a fearsome amount of power to wield.

The feminine in her fullness is driven by the instinct to give life to others. She is fertile, abundant, and is sending out a constant signal to the field that she is ready to create more and share what she has. Her service is being in alignment with the force of creation that's moving through her, and showing her exactly where she needs to be of service, which is not always what she thinks it is.

Service is not overextending yourself or compromising yourself to please others. It's not about renouncing your desires or giving up your personal authority.

Your turn on is your service.

Your creative fire is your service.

Your alignment is your service.

When you're overflowing with your feminine energy, you're naturally going to be of service to the world, whether it be just into walking into a shopping centre or signing a deal.

People will feel your frequency of alignment and ease, and that will move something in them.

There've been times where I've been at complete disservice, even if I've been of service to people because I've been exhausted. It's not a good place to serve from, actually. You can do more harm than good serving from that place.

Sometimes in that space, the greatest service you can be is to extract your energy from others and what you would draw and nourish yourself to the point where you're over overflowing again.

When I'm stuck in my mind, feeling sorry for myself, like I'm not valuable or I've got nothing to offer the world, sometimes the most powerful thing I can do is to go down to a local deli, buy someone in the shop a coffee, and be of service in some small way, which brings me back to my heart again. From there, I gently slip back into the flow.

When I'm going through a massive training or a program, and I'm feeling fucking bogged down and dead, I go out and

I treat everyone or go and buy everyone a gift, get everyone coffee, and it's like I'm overflowing again. Just from dropping myself back into a state of service and out of this feeling of victimhood. The truth is, the love we want is always there. We just have to serve it. We serve love, it serves us.

In my adult life, I've had to do a lot of repatterning around associating service with doing something big for the collective.

As a child, every morning, I would go and pick lavender and take it to everyone in the street. And it was just the best way to start my day. I'd go to school feeling excited because I had given a gift to all my neighbours.

When I was living in India, in these little communities that had nothing, where people were just in service to one another, everyone was happy.

Service doesn't have to be grandiose.

As someone that feels the collective sphere so deeply and feels that I have to do something big in order to create change and save the planet, I have news for you. The planet's fine; we're the ones who are fucked. She's a self-sustaining organism. She's fine without us. We need to resolve our own trauma. Only then can we serve from an internal place of authentic heart connection, and that's what serves her.

You can logically be showing up and have this amazing non-for-profit that serves the earth and then do all the right things by the book, and really not be of service because you're not connecting to your heart.

When we find that centre point of the heart internally within ourselves, that's when we're truly serving and our business can grow in harmony with the Earth, because we're no longer needing her. We're no longer extracting from her because we're self-regulating our own energy.

Your business is a manifestation of your heart and an extension of that space. If your business is disconnected from your heart, it will not serve anyone.

And when it is, it becomes the most magnificent, life-giving garden that nourishes everyone whom it touches.

BREAST MASSAGE PRACTICE TO OPEN THE HEART

The feminine is biologically wired so that her sexual energy opens naturally when her heart is open. In order to have a wildly alive, ecstatic business and relationship, it is important that are our hearts are open and receptive.

Like a flower, our heart opens in response to nourishment, care, and love.

Breast massage is a powerful practice I use and prescribe to keep the heartspace open and heart energy circulating throughout the rest of the body.

Whether you have breasts or not, taking time to massage and care for your chest and heartspace will do wonders for the energetics of your heart and your business.

Just like with any other practice, enter and cleanse your sacred space.

Grant yourself the use of body oils if you desire. Rose, geranium, thyme, ylang.

Touch, massage, and listen to your breasts. Do not have an agenda; move with tenderness and care. Breast tissue is incredibly sensitive and holds a lot of emotion. Emotion can also become lodged in the ribs and the sternum. The entire chest wants to be touched, loved, and cared for, in order to open up the full capacity of the heart.

Give yourself this gift and watch what happens.

CHAPTER TEN
Scaling Your Wild Business™

The way that we scale our Wild Business™ is by harnessing the connections in our community.

My work has been supported by incredible teammates and partners at every stage of my business growth, who have not only helped me achieve my vision but who have tapped into this frequency for themselves and created businesses of their own. Our team focuses on deep listening, anchored in the heart of the feminine.

Scaling your Wild Business™ is ultimately about building other leaders who are empowered to think and feel for themselves.

Within just six months of starting up, my business grew to six figures – with no HR department, no strategy, and no overthinking.

All I've had to do was embody my frequency, put out my vibrational signals, and respond to the people who are attracted to my call.

When your business is ready to grow and scale, you will know. It will start to require more than just you to bring your vision to life.

CREATING LEADERS

As a leader, you have to have people to lead. You have to have a team. You have to have community. Your team needs to be comprised of people that are attuned to the same way of doing things as you, or who can be easily attuned to your way.

There are some people who have come into my business, whose psychic abilities and feminine creativity haven't been natural to them, but they've been initiated just by coming into the field of the business and being open to it. I haven't actually had to do anything myself. It's like the business entity itself chose them and opened them up, and now they understand it, and now they listen. They can actually hear the same frequency that comes through me, they also pick up on the downloads that I get.

Our team meetings are based upon deep listening. We have monthly deep listening calls where the focus is asking, "What's present and alive?" From there, we uncover where are we individually not aligned, and how can we shift that so that the ecosystem is flowing. With a team of any size, if one person is off, the whole thing is off.

Your commitment as a leader is not just a commitment to, "Oh, this is the way that I want to do business." It's the commitment to every single person that's a part of the business and listening to their channel, too.

Yesterday, I had my saleswoman message me saying, "The people coming to inquire about the program are blocked. They're not committing." She's like, "What's going on?"

My sense immediately was that she was personally blocked by a feeling of shame around selling a high ticketed program. I suggested she do a particular energetic clearing technique on this block, and she said, "Yeah, that was my sense." After she shifted her energy, the program started to fill.

If one person's out, then the whole field is blocked, and every single one of us feel it because we're all established in the ecosystem. We're a part of it. Someone's energy off and unclear is like having a kink in the pipes.

When it comes to scaling your team, the Wild Business™ model creates leaders, not followers. It empowers your team to think and feel for themselves. My teammates, with their own unique gifts, skills, and intuitive abilities, are just as capable as me of hearing what the business requires and taking action. We all trust each other because we're all tuned in to the same psychic channel.

All of the staff members that work under me have taken my programs, and so have a refined and strong intuitive ability – something that is a prerequisite to working within my business. If each person within your team is psychically awake and can tune into the deeper layers of consciousness beyond the mind, it takes the pressure off of you to make all of the decisions, as your team won't need as much direction.

In order to be a strong leader of a movement, you need to be psychically switched on and intuitively aligned to your business and to those that are in it.

The way to do that is to first ensure that your intuition is alive and awake, using the rituals and practices I teach in this book and then, to teach the others in your team how to cultivate and work with their own intuitive abilities too. To work with practices that shift the state of consciousness of the eco-system, the team, and the business itself in order for the flow to be restored again.

I have designed a short course, the Wild Business™ LEADERSHIP COURSE, which I train my team members in. It provides them with the subconscious clearing tools, such as Kinesiology and emotional clearing, to be able to clear their own inner blocks to show up. I've given them all the tools to clear themselves. So, they'll just go off and they'll do a little emotional clear using kinesiology and they're like, "Oh, I'm good now." Then they're flowing. Then the clients come in, and the whole ecosystem flows.

If you are wanting to steep in this knowledge for yourself in order to transmit it to others, come on board to the Wild Business™ training, which you can find on our website, www.wildbusiness.com.

Weaving the Web

Your business scales itself through connection and communi-ty. The moment I realized this was the moment I left my last ever job in the hospital system, having discovered that I was a medical intuitive. All I could think was, *I'm just walking away. I'm moving to Melbourne. I have no idea what to do.*

When I landed in Melbourne, I didn't know anyone in the city. One day I was scrolling through social media on Face-book, and I was just so drawn to this one particular person. I reached out and asked her to go to coffee. This is after I had a vision of working with men, doing Tantric work. I met up with her, and basically asked her, "What do you do? Who are you?" And she's like, "I'm a Tantric practitioner, I own a studio with rooms that I rent out to other practitioners, and I train practitioners too."

And I was like, "Oh. Here's the thing."

She was my connection to that work, which I did for a few years. From there, I was drawn to this person or that person, each of whom had a piece for my growth. It's not about doing it alone. It's not about figuring anything out that you don't have knowledge of. It's about connection and community more than anything.

Astrologically, we've moved out of the Age of Pisces, which is the age of the mystic, the guru, and the spiritual leader. It's about someone showing you the way. It's about information downloading through one person as a stream of consciousness to others. Pisces is the Mother Teresa, it's the one that actually plays the role of the savior in some sense.

Now, we are moving into the Age of Aquarius, awakened to the fact that everyone has that spark of enlightenment inside of themselves, and we learn and grow by sharing our gifts with one another.

It's no longer about going into an ashram and following a lineage and being under a guru and one particular teacher and then outsourcing the knowledge. It's about following the thread of connections in our lives and then weaving the web of our world where everyone benefits. When you meet people you are meant to grow and scale with, you will know. There is a resonance. When you meet them, there's an energetic exchange and an opportunity to be curious about what you can co-create together. If we can find that point of resonance where our frequencies are aligned and it feels easy and natural to be in harmony, creation flows.

That's how it works in Wild Business™, and it's how this movement was born. In 2019, I had this massive journey around doing a ceremony to release my role as a healer to step into full authorship. I had a raven wing and a drum that signified this healer role, so I gave them away, and I called in a new raven to come into my life. I imagined it would be another wing that would show up on my travels, but then Raven, the writer, showed up in my inbox, bringing the spark of inspiration that became Wild Business™.

I thought, "Oh, that's the raven I called in." It wasn't what I expected, but it was organic and aligned. And, as the universe would have it, I not only created a movement and stepped fully into my authorship, but I received another raven wing just a few months later.

I have a lot of fun with this, because the way I connect with my community is I just listen to who's in my psychic field, I chat to them online and something opens up, and then opportunities always come from that. I've just been playing with that more this past week and actually realizing how much I love it.

Scaling is largely dependent on our ability to surrender to the flow of life and surrender to understanding that there is this mycelial network, and this web, and that our ability to connect in and weave the web is going to actually fuel into, or take from, our ability to weave a business and have success.

My life force comes from my ability to give and receive constantly in my environment and with my connections, and to have that symbiotic relationship with my community.

As a leader moving forwards, we have to be aware of how we are influenced by the ecosystem of our body of work and our entity, how every single person feeds back into that entity. We need to attune to our deepest intuition so that we can hear what's happening within the ecosystem and respond in ways that support a state of harmony, or balance, or syntropy.

Scaling your Wild Business™ is not about planning anything out. It's a continuation of the practice of simply listening. When we get out of the way and stop trying to make things happen or make our business grow, our impulses are clearer and we can follow them one after another. These impulses will lead us to the people we need to meet who can help us achieve our vision. When we are stable in this frequency, we can scale our teams and our revenue with ease.

The vortex and the portal of your business will keep growing and growing over time, attracting more and more experiences that are aligned with your soul. Enjoy every moment! As your entrepreneurial career evolves, the struggles that you face now will one day be the lessons you look back on with gratitude. Your main task is to stay connected to your heart and keep listening deeply to the voice of your intuition. Serve love, and let love serve you.

Everything will happen from there.

Practice: Serve Small

The next time you need an instant boost of heart-opening love, do something that's of service for another in a really little way. Make a bed, leave a note, buy a coffee, fold a t-shirt.

See what happens.

CHAPTER ELEVEN
Join the Wild Business™ Movement

Wild one, this is just the beginning – of doing less than you ever have before.

And receiving more.

If you've traveled through these pages, you are already weaving the web of your Wild Business™.

Your soul blueprint and essence is landing.

You don't need to do anything – just trust what you already know.

At the Vancouver Peace Summit in 2009, the Dalai Lama said, "The world will be saved by the western woman."

I believe the world does not need to be saved. We need to save ourselves from the belief that everything external to us constantly needs "saving," and to begin with ourselves – otherwise we will be eternally feeding victim consciousness via the externalization of our own power. We certainly *have* created a sh*t show where it is supposedly normal to walk around, completely disconnected from one another in the pursuit of some kind of "American dream;" a fantasy of fulfillment that we're always seeking, not realizing it's right here, present right now, in the ecstasy of our bodies and connection to nature.

And I do believe the world will be bought back into a deeper form of balance through the fourth wave of feminism and the rising of the feminine so that she leads and he follows.

So that our empathy, our intuition, and our emotional connection are at the forefront, and systems and structures are in place to support this, over control, greed, and the raping and pillaging of resources of the Earth.

The new world will be created by leaders who are connected to the spirit of the feminine within them; who honour their heart and their sexuality, and who are radiating that life force into their business.

Business is powerful and must be respected as a vehicle to drive change. We have the choice to start creating businesses with more consciousness. We can only make our greatest contribution to this planet when we are giving from our fullness, from our thriving. When we are living our wild nature, breathing ecstasy, feeling deeply, and trusting ourselves.

This book was born from my desire to see you rise into the leadership that you are here to bring.

The world needs your feminine power now more than ever.

I know and feel in my heart that we all want to live and create from a place of passion and aliveness. We all want to be aligned in our truth, our soul purpose, and our essence.

Know that you're not alone – I am here to support you at every phase of your journey.

The Wild Business™ movement is *our* movement.

My team and I have been crafting a whole new sphere of resources and training to help you land your genius, channel your business, and use the feminine frequency formula to become the unique, brilliant business leader that you are.

I predict that these next years will bring about a new wave of artists, spiritual entrepreneurs, and activists whose voices will change the course of human history.

We are ripe for evolution on all levels as a society, and it's time to evolve along with Nature into a state of higher harmony. We are here to create from our joy, move with power, share our frequency, and live our truth.

We're not here to do things traditionally.

We're not here to replicate a model that's already out there.

We're here to pave a new way forwards in business that works for the futurists and revolutionaries that cannot stand fitting into a map or a model that takes from their sovereignty and power.

This work is for the people that are prepared to take risks. Those that do not overthink things or try and box their creativity into a strategy.

It's about radically trusting in the feminine. Radically trusting in nature. And it's about trusting that your frequency has the power to move mountains.

When you opened this book, you opened a portal to miracles.

You already know what you're here to do.

Now you have a way to get there.

At the end of the day, if you're going to show up for anything, don't show up for "work" – show up for whatever takes
you home to your soul. And the work will do itself.

Let your intuition guide you now.

To your Wild Business™,

Sigourney

Special Note

One of the principles of Wild Business™ is about the circulation of resources and finances back into philanthropic projects and purposes. Money is a resource that yields great power. It is not evil. It has just been used to serve purposes that have extracted the divine for far too long now.

This book will donate proceeds back into reforestation projects that support Earth regeneration.

About the Author

Sigourney Belle is on a mission to revolutionize the way we do business – bringing it back to the heart of the feminine. Creator of multiple six-figure global companies herself, she has seen firsthand what it takes to thrive in a traditionally masculine environment while staying connected to her desire, intuition, and creative genius. Sigourney will show you that when you tap into your wild nature, you can create a business that is both successful and nourishing to your body, mind, heart, and spirit.

Acknowledgements

I would like to acknowledge everyone who has been deeply involved in the journey of launching this book into the world.

To the team by my side; to my Publisher, Andréa and her team; and to Raven, who has been here every step of the journey.

Made in the USA
Las Vegas, NV
19 March 2021